19 - T's inability to appeal to transcendence for Eng. Canada
21 - whereas Fr. Canada has "an abundance of history and myth"
(56 - pristine = my textbook too)
66 - liberalism = pure form
[interesting combination of biography & critique]

Canadian Biography Series

99
68ff - Canadian identity a problem for liberalism [Christiano vs. Trudeau]
81, 83 - early Trudeau reform - divorce, consensual sex

PIERRE ELLIOTT TRUDEAU:

REASON BEFORE PASSION

1919 -
P.M. June '68-
m. Mar. '71

85 - Trudeau's god delusion [?]
100ff - T's principles
139 - summary of critique

*Trudeau, fifteenth prime minister
of Canada, in Winnipeg, 1981.*

Pierre Elliott Trudeau

REASON BEFORE PASSION

Kevin J. Christiano

ECW PRESS

Copyright © ECW PRESS, 1994

CANADIAN CATALOGUING IN PUBLICATION DATA

Christiano, Kevin J.
Pierre Elliott Trudeau : reason before passion

Includes bibliographical references.
ISBN 1-55022-188-4

1. Trudeau, Pierre Elliott, 1919– . 2. Prime
ministers – Canada – Biography. I. Title.

FC626.T88C5 1994   971.064 4 092   C94-930010-1
FI034.3.T88C5 1993

This book has been published with the assistance of the Ministry
of Culture, Tourism and Recreation of the Province of Ontario,
through funds provided by the Ontario Publishing Centre, and with
the assistance of grants from the Department of Communications,
The Canada Council, the Ontario Arts Council, and the Government
of Canada through the Canadian Studies and Special Projects
Directorate of the Department of the Secretary of State of Canada.

Design and imaging by ECW Type & Art, Oakville, Ontario.
Printed by Imprimerie Gagné, Louiseville, Québec.

Distributed by General Distribution Services,
30 Lesmill Road, Toronto, Ontario M3B 2T6.
(416) 445-3333, (800) 387-0172 (Canada), FAX (416) 445-5967.

Distributed to the trade in the United States exclusively
by InBook, 140 Commerce Street, P.O. Box 120261,
East Haven, Connecticut, U.S.A. 06512,
(203) 467-4257, FAX (203) 469-8364.
Customer service: (800) 243-0138, FAX (800) 334-3892.

Published by ECW PRESS,
2120 Queen Street East,
Toronto, Ontario M4E 1E2.

ACKNOWLEDGEMENTS

The condensed format of a work such as this precludes an extensive list of acknowledgements. Yet there are several people whose contributions to this effort have been so substantial that to ignore them would be worse than negligent.

Calum M. Carmichael of Carleton University was instrumental by being a constant audience for my ideas about Pierre Trudeau and Canadian politics. These verbal forays ordinarily occurred during what became regular visits to his office, library, and home — evidence enough for his status as a reliable colleague and trusted friend.

Catherine Lecco Stern, a native of Prince Edward Island, has from our time together in graduate school been an instructive critic of my views about Canadian society. A more pleasant adversary would be hard for any author to find. Here in Indiana, another dislocated Canadian, D'A. Jonathan D. Boulton, generously encouraged my growing interest in his country. George A. Rawlyk of Queen's University ploughed through an early draft of this book, uprooted many weeds, and left behind some seed as well. Rare is the scholar who can match his style of combining rigorous commentary with gracious credit.

Numerous suggestions (ranging in tone from prods to insistences), gestures of support, and occasional congratulations came my way from, among others, Reginald W. Bibby, Johanna Froehlich, Wendy Griswold, Robert T. Handy, Nathan O. Hatch, Flynt Leverett, Robert C. Liebman, Martin E. Marty, Mark A. Noll, Roger O'Toole, Stephen P. Rounds, Mark Stanton, John F. Wilson, and Marsha Witten. To this day, Robert Wuthnow furnishes sound direction and potent inspiration.

On the more practical side, I must mention the unaccountably conscientious Ruth Morin and the able staff at Books Canada on Sparks Street in Ottawa. In response to sometimes nervous inquiries and seemingly endless orders, they kept newly released Canadian books moving to an author based far to the south (and thus deprived of timely access to most of this material). My attempts to redress (over the telephone, no less) the stubborn imbalance in cross-border shopping were met consistently with good advice and cheer.

What I could not buy immediately from Canadian booksellers I obtained ultimately through the persistence of Linda K. Gregory and the other personnel in the Interlibrary Loan office of the Theodore M. Hesburgh Library at the University of Notre Dame. Although my appearances in their doorway invariably signalled more work for them, these dedicated librarians always greeted me with a smile.

Most of the illustrations for this book were culled from collections administered by the Documentary Art and Photography Division of the National Archives of Canada. The expert staff of the Archives (including Hélène Godda, Sheila Mendonça, Roanne Mokhtar, Micheline Robert, Andrew Roger, and Brian Turner) answered my questions fully and prepared photographic prints speedily. In addition, I owe a special debt of gratitude to Helen De Roia of the Collections Consultation Unit. During one of my research trips to the national capital in July 1992, Ms. De Roia offered patient and attentive service as I sorted through the Archives' voluminous holdings of unpublished photographs of Trudeau, his family, and his colleagues.

They probably do not endorse parts of what follows, but George Costaris and Mary Lynn Becker of the Canadian Consulate General in Detroit helped nevertheless by trying ceaselessly to integrate me into the vibrant academic subculture of Canadian studies in the United States.

James C. Cavendish, Melvin F. Hall, Jina Paik, and Marek Szopski provided assistance with library research at different stages of this project, while the Department of Sociology at Princeton University (through the good offices of its chairman, Marvin Bressler, and its administrative assistant, Cynthia Gibson) extended various visiting privileges to me.

Portions of this biography were published as an article in the *Dalhousie Review*. I thank the editor, Alan Andrews, and the publisher, Dalhousie University Press, for granting me permission to reprint that essay in revised form here. I also thank the University of Toronto Press for permission to reprint a portion of Trudeau's *Conversation with Canadians*, a compilation of speeches.

A small materials grant from the Institute for Scholarship in the Liberal Arts of the College of Arts and Letters at Notre Dame helped to defray the cost of reproducing the illustrations for this book.

PHOTOGRAPHS: Cover photo, Robert Cooper, Office of the Prime Minister, © National Archives of Canada, is used by permission of National Archives of Canada / PA-184562; frontispiece illustration, Robert Cooper, Office of the Prime Minister, © National Archives of Canada, is used by permission of National Archives of Canada/PA-184564; illustration 2, McGee, *Montreal Star*, is used by permission of National Archives of Canada/PA-134512; illustration 3, Robert Cooper, Office of the Prime Minister, © National Archives of Canada, is used by permission of National Archives of Canada/PA-140705; illustration 4, *Weekend Magazine*, is used by permission of National Archives of Canada/PA-115081; illustration 5, Walter Curtin, © National Archives of Canada, is used by permission of National Archives of Canada/PA-137103; illustration 6, © *Gazette* [Montreal], is used by permission of National Archives of Canada/PA-117502; illustration 7, © Hydro-Quebec, is used by permission of National Archives of Canada/PA-185291; illustration 8, Duncan Cameron, © National Archives of Canada, is used by permission of National Archives of Canada/PA-117107; illustration 9, Horst Ehricht, *Maclean's*, © National Archives of Canada, is used by permission of National Archives of Canada/PA-184614; illustration 10, Duncan Cameron, © National Archives of Canada, is used by permission of National Archives of Canada/PA-111213; illustration 11, Brosseau, *Montreal Star*, is used by permission of National Archives of Canada/PA-163903; illustration 12, Robert Cooper, Office of the Prime Minister, © National Archives of Canada, is used by permission of National Archives of Canada/PA-184570; illustration 13, Robert Cooper, Office of the Prime Minister, © National Archives of Canada, is used by permission of National Archives of Canada/PA-184566; illustration 14, Robert Cooper, Office of the Prime Minister, © National Archives of Canada, is used by permission of National Archives of Canada/PA-184567; illustrations 15 and 16, Robert Cooper, Office of the Prime Minister, © National Archives of Canada, are used by permission of National Archives of Canada/PA-184568 and PA-184569; illustration 17, © Bruce Harlan, is used by permission of the University of Notre Dame; illustration 18, Marcos Townsend, CANAPRESS Photo Service, is used by permission of the Canadian Press.

TABLE OF CONTENTS

LIST OF ILLUSTRATIONS

Pierre Elliott Trudeau

REASON BEFORE PASSION

INTRODUCTION

"The past is not dead," argued the Nobel laureate William
Faulkner, "it is not even past." Like the brooding sectional
history that dominates the southern author's novels, rever-
berations from the life of Pierre Elliott Trudeau have not died.
Nor have they merged silently into the long, sleepy story of the
Canadian past. Although a political generation has arrived and
departed since the missionary zeal of "the three doves," the
vocal defiance of "Vive le Québec . . . libre!," the popular silli-
ness of "Trudeaumania," and Margaret and the two Christmas
nativities, one can only repeat the opening words of Stephen
Clarkson and Christina McCall in their two-volume biography
of Trudeau: "He haunts us still."

Pierre Trudeau is a presence so large, a figure so formidable,
an influence so constitutive of current political debate in Canada,
that it could not be otherwise. "To understand Canada in the late
twentieth century," Reg Whitaker writes, "it is necessary to
understand both Trudeau's ideas and his politics." Andrew Stark
concurs: "The power that ideas held over the man, the dominance
that the man held over his government, and the influence of that
government on a generation," he says, "make an understanding
of Trudeau's political thought necessary to an understanding of
the current crisis" in Canadian politics.

How else can we account for the fact that in a swan-song
appearance before a hastily assembled band of Tories, Prime

Minister Brian Mulroney, with a nine-year legacy to protect, chose not to fire parting shots at his many contemporary foes? Instead, as Susan Delacourt puts it in "Legacy Distorted," the "clear and unflinching target" of his volleys was Trudeau, who held no formal position during that period, and who expressed himself solely through a trickle of editorial comments, personal essays, public testimony, and the occasional after-dinner remark.

Trudeau's opinions still carry enormous weight in Canadian society; seldom have so few words mattered so much to so many, if newsstand sales and best-seller lists are indicative. Despite Delacourt's claim of "a raging grudge against Mr. Trudeau," Mulroney embraced his record as the gold standard in prime ministerial performance: "All of Mr. Mulroney's self-positioning for the history books is being done with Mr. Trudeau in mind. Whatever Mr. Trudeau did, Mr. Mulroney wants to be seen as the man who did it better. . . ."

Throughout Trudeau's long public career, his motto was *"la raison avant la passion"* ("reason before passion"), displayed on a wall hanging in his official residence. Yet few Canadians of the twentieth century have evoked as much raw emotion — whether political enthusiasm or individual ire — as Trudeau. Many run-of-the-mill politicians make enemies, but Trudeau is someone whose philosophical rigidity and personal reserve taxed even those who otherwise agreed with him. "I never thought," confesses the novelist W.P. Kinsella in "Voices of the Nation," advocating a "No" vote in the national referendum on the Charlottetown constitutional agreement, "that I'd be on the same side of anything as that little weasel, Pierre Trudeau."

This brief biography of Pierre Trudeau attempts to explain some of the reasons for these special reactions. All the same, its brevity dictates that it cannot function as a comprehensive chronicle of Trudeau's public acts. Most of all, this is not a systematic analysis of federal policy under Canada's fifteenth prime minister, nor is it an assessment of him in his capacity as a practical politician. Students of Canadian government and public administration can find bibliographical information on a variety of such works listed in the back of this one. In contrast, this book adopts a broader and in some ways more personal focus. Most simply, it is an attempt to trace the development of Trudeau's self and his thinking against the backdrop of a pivotal era in Canadian history, the latter two-thirds of what was once hopefully dubbed "the Canadian century."

Without actually occupying the space within Trudeau's head, it is impossible to say with certainty what motivates him. Nevertheless, this book tries to convey, through inferences from the abundant stock of his words and deeds, some of what the former prime minister must have felt and thought over the course of a life like no other in his country's history. Regardless of his role as a historical actor, however, Trudeau is primarily a thinker. His intellect, in fact, was his paramount contribution to Canadian politics. Throughout these pages, accordingly, the narrative emphasis is on what Trudeau was thinking, and on how what he did in a particular instance reflected what he believed. On fundamental issues, these connections are usually quite direct; after all, Trudeau has been nothing if not consistent in framing, explaining, and sometimes imposing his personal creed.

But to observe that Trudeau has acted with notable consistency is not to say that he is therefore someone who is easy to understand — let alone that he is a person with whom everyone can sympathize. Indeed, he is an exceptional man, in the literal sense of that word. Moreover, there is an undercurrent of tragedy in the telling of Trudeau's life story: tragedy here meaning not that he has suffered a uniformly unhappy or rueful existence, but that his biography is tragic in the mode of heroes from the literature of classical antiquity. Such heroes come to represent their ages at the same time that they transcend them; they stand apart from the sources out of which they spring, serving simultaneously as the least typical examples of their origins and as their most authentic emblems.

Time and again in sagas of nobility and shame, these heroes gather up the energies within their essentially solitary selves and project them boldly into the battle — to discharge a duty, to right a wrong, to defend an idea, to save a nation. The tragedy of the story arrives with the realization that their causes are doomed, not by a shortage of strength or bravery but by opportunities overlooked and choices not made, by flaws that are as much a part of their identity as is their skill in the fight.

Like the great characters of literary tragedy, Trudeau fought courageously and without restraint. Yet his efforts merely bought limited time against a challenge of nationhood that could adequately be met only through a marriage of philosophical precept and political vision that he would not conscion. For Trudeau, as for the tragic heroes of national epics the world over, the same brand of fervour that he summoned for the contest prevented, in the end, its true resolution.

CHOOSING CANADA

In May 1980, Canada was in crisis. Ostensibly a model of tranquillity and stability, it faced a severe threat to its integrity. Just three months earlier, former Prime Minister Pierre Trudeau returned from a premature retirement when the nine-month rule of Joe Clark, the hapless Conservative leader, ended in electoral defeat. New elections were provoked when his government failed on a budget vote in the House of Commons late the previous year.

Trudeau returned to power, however, only to face another election. This time it was confined to his home province of Quebec, but it had implications for the future of North America. It signified, in the words of Jean Chrétien in "Bringing the Constitution Home," "the political confrontation of the century in Canada." Quebec was seeking the dignity of nationhood via "sovereignty-association," or independence in political affairs but close cooperation with Canada in economic and military matters. The ruling separatist Parti québécois (PQ) was going to

FIGURE 2

*On the campaign trail, May 1979: Trudeau presents
the Liberal government's case to Montreal voters
during his only unsuccessful election campaign.*

the people, asking in a plebiscite on 20 May for a mandate to begin negotiations with the federal government about this autonomous status. Before long, the Quebec government's skilful manipulation of the hallowed symbols of a nation-in-the-making gave the campaign "the mystique of a holy war," as Robert Sheppard and Michael Valpy phrase it.

Trudeau and the federal ministers from Quebec pulled out all the stops to defeat the separatist initiative. Their efforts climaxed with a speech that Trudeau gave on 14 May 1980, less than a week before the balloting. Still drained from the national campaign in February that had restored the Liberal Party to a majority in the Commons, Trudeau marshalled his energies to save Canada.

On the night of his address, in the Paul Sauvé Arena in Montreal, he stood before a throng of Quebeckers more as a historical symbol than as a political figure. As Clarkson and McCall put it, he was "a fighter, an activist, a patriot who had travelled the world and conquered it but had come home because Quebec was what mattered most to him, a man who contradicted parochial nationalism by his very being, showing in his person what a Quebecker could achieve in a larger Canada." Nevertheless, this symbol delivered a political speech that Sheppard and Valpy judge to have been "an electrifying performance that reverberated throughout the province for days"; its dual highlights were a pledge to the people of Quebec and a warning to other Canadians:

I know that I can make a most solemn commitment that following a "No" vote we will immediately take action to renew the constitution and we will not stop until we have done that.

And I make a solemn declaration to all Canadians in the other provinces: we, the Quebec MPs, are laying ourselves on the line, because we are telling Quebeckers to vote "No" and telling you in the other provinces that we will not agree to your interpreting a "No" vote as an indication that everything is fine and can remain as it was before.

We want change and we are willing to lay our seats in the House on the line to have change.

When the ballots were counted, the "No" side had won the support of nearly three in five adults (59.5%) who had participated in the referendum. Although French-speaking Quebeckers were about evenly split over the allure of sovereignty, the voters of Quebec as a group sided with Canada and constitutional reform. Trudeau and company then took up the constitutional fight with zeal. "For the prime minister and the team he gathered around him," according to Sheppard and Valpy, the struggle "had messianic purpose": to fashion "symbols that would give the country — like the tinman of Oz — a heart."

But the hoped-for innovations — a domicile in Canada for the constitution, recognition of language protections in all provinces, and a bill of individual rights — are not so much symbols as consequences of the presumed power of symbols to convince others of their necessity. As goals of political discussion, they presuppose a set of national symbols that, as the ensuing debates demonstrated, Canada could not pretend that it had.

FATHER OF A NEW CONFEDERATION

In April 1982, Prime Minister Trudeau presided over the signing of a new Canadian constitution. This document, born of an unstable marriage between lofty ideals and practical politics, was the crowning achievement of his public life. The new constitution ended the last legal vestige of Canada's outgrown status as a colony, the old British North America (BNA) Act.

First approved by the English parliament in 1867, the BNA Act had served for over a century as the constitution of Canada, even though it contained no clear definition of Canadian citizenship, no list of the rights and obligations pertaining thereto, and no

FIGURE 3

Signing the new Constitution: as Prime Minister Trudeau
holds the parchment steady, Queen Elizabeth II signs the
Constitution Act in April 1982. It contains the Charter of
Rights and Freedoms, a product of Trudeau's lifelong advocacy
of individual liberty. Watching, to Her Majesty's left, are
Michael Pitfield and Michael Kirby, key advisors to Trudeau.

method of amendment short of further resort to the parliament at Westminster. The Constitution Act that replaced it addressed these deficiencies, notably by repatriating its essential provisions in a domestically forged agreement, and entrenching within it a comprehensive Charter of Rights and Freedoms.

Yet the man most responsible for the new constitution had fought during his entire political life against others who sought to give Canada and its people a determinate meaning. Raised in a setting in which adherence to tradition meant submission to autocracy and anti-intellectualism, Trudeau pursued instead an unwavering insistence on reason. Tested in a political culture emptied by history and circumstance of unifying elements, he attempted to create a nation by vigorously defending the federal union that joins the country's many fragments.

Unfortunately for Trudeau, nations are not reasoned into being. They issue forth as the products not of dialogue but of history. Around the facts of history are arrayed songs of noble and daring deeds, stories of virtue under trial, and claims to uniqueness among the peoples of the earth. These items form the symbolic substance of nationhood. This substance may be augmented with difficulty, but it is denigrated or denied at peril to the nation itself.

Trudeau appreciated this reality more acutely perhaps than any Canadian of his generation. But his convictions as a liberal prevented him from acting purposefully on his knowledge. To the contrary, much of his public energy was spent trying to render illegitimate any impulse toward a "religious" (as opposed to a rational) response to the collective concerns of the people.

Trudeau provides an exemplary case study of the fate of intelligent politicians and committed leaders when they do not or cannot situate state action in history and motivate its acceptance by appeal to a transcendent plane. In Canada, without what social scientists (e.g., Robert Bellah) call a "civil religion" upon which to draw, Trudeau could gain only so much security for himself and his country. By the end of his time in office, he had managed to rid Canada of the last tatters of colonial rule and bring it to political maturity. He had managed, too, in a vaunted drive for "French power," to bring some of the brightest and most able Quebec politicians into central positions in the federal system. But his intentional yet unavoidable neglect to ground these accomplishments in something symbolic may ironically have made hopes for a true Canadian nation more precarious than ever.

THE TRIALS OF
TRUE PATRIOT LOVE

Biography is history recounted in the story of a single life. In order to fathom the life of so ardent a federalist as Pierre Trudeau, we must understand not only the political system in which he functioned for almost two decades during his career in government, but also (and perhaps more importantly) the political culture against which he formed his elementary principles as a public man.

If we are accustomed to viewing the younger Trudeau as a dashing assailant of tradition, then it is perhaps awkward to label him a reactionary. Yet a reactionary he is: he has set himself squarely against what time has put before him. The conservative philosopher George Grant grasped, early in the years of the Trudeau government, how much of the prime minister's thought and behaviour were of this nature. "Throughout his career his appeals have been to universalism," Grant observed in 1971;

In Mr. Trudeau's writings there is evident distaste for what was by tradition his own, and what is put up along with that distaste are universalist goods which will be capable of dissolving that tradition. Indeed this quality of being a convert to modern liberalism is one cause of his formidability. Most English-speaking liberals have lived in universalism much longer. They have not come to it out of something different, but have grown up in it as their tradition. They are apt, therefore, either to accept it automatically or even to start to be cynical about its ability to solve human problems. On the other hand, Mr. Trudeau's espousal has behind it the force of his distaste of its opposite against which he is reacting. Recent converts are especially effective exponents of a system because they have the confidence of believing they are doing right.

We should remember moreover, that both Trudeau's native surroundings and the broader culture that he later entered have been unable to furnish Canada with a national ideology that works, that opens itself to outsiders as it unites those already under its sway. Although these two nullities are equally weak, they exist for different reasons.

The political imagination of anglophone Canada could not compose a viable civic myth from the few effective symbols at its disposal: anachronistic shreds of imperial pomp and a largely misplaced loyalty to the British crown. Their former grandeur had long ago collapsed into a seamy colonialism where it had not vanished altogether. Whereas English speakers in Canada lack raw material for the construction of a truly national faith, French Canadians possess an abundance of history and myth. Yet they, too, have trouble answering the call to bring meaning to the idea of Canada. While the diminishing federalist presence in the French population promotes enthusiasm for the Canadian state, its appeals do not resonate with abiding popular symbols. Separatists, on the other hand, have many of the emotional insignia of nationhood but no inclination to cede them to the service of the central government.

Quebec, its motto proclaims, remembers (*"Je me souviens"*). But like an aged and increasingly cranky relative in the family of Confederation, Quebec may remember too much. And, like a senile relative, it remembers selectively and sometimes mal-evolently, recalling episodes of collective frustration that breed historical resentment. Such memories hold little promise of binding Canadians together; the contrary force is what they produce. "Well, one thing is certain," Hugh MacLennan remarks through a character in his landmark novel, *Two Solitudes* (1945). "The same brand of patriotism is never likely to exist all over Canada" because "Each race so violently disapproves of the tribal gods of the other. . . ."

Two recent examples from Canadian politics point out how prone to division is a plural society with too keen a historical memory. The late René Lévesque, premier of Quebec under the separatist Parti québécois, describes in his memoirs his schoolboy studies, including a course in history. Having read with excitement about the adventures of Pierre d'Iberville and other brave soldiers and settlers of New France, Lévesque complains,

it was downhill all the way to the Plains of Abraham. It was all over. From then on somebody else's history began, the history of another country we didn't feel like learning, with the exception of Montgomery and his gang, and Arnold the turncoat, who came close to reannexing us to the continent, which would have taken care of the question of free trade forever. Even Benjamin Franklin, however, had to give up on the idea when faced with our colonial loyalty so soon transferred to the British. . . . It was all over, all right. And for years to come.

In a way, Jean Chrétien agrees, but draws the opposite conclusion from Lévesque's history lesson. Chrétien, a native of Quebec, was the federal minister of justice at the time of the province's plebiscite on sovereignty-association in May 1980. Pleading for a *"non"* vote from his fellow French Canadians, Chrétien nonetheless acknowledged the burden of historical memory while trying to discount it. "Quebeckers," he confesses in *Straight from the Heart*, "have wanted to rewrite history ever since their ancestors lost the tiny battle on the Plains of Abraham because the English troops crept up on them in the night."

Recalling the referendum campaign, Chrétien admits, " 'I, too, wish I had been able to wake up Montcalm and tell him the English were coming,' I used to say in my speeches, 'but I was not there.' The audiences laughed, but it was my way of making the serious point that we had to face reality." Quebec's refusal, at least before 1980, to "face reality" made for "good art" but "lousy thought." His view may account for the precision with which perceptions of Quebec's conduct in national affairs oscillate between a brilliance that the others selfishly ignore and a self-destructiveness that some perversely applaud.

Trudeau is a son of Quebec in the dual sense of affinity and ineluctability that any claim of kinship implies. As a French Canadian, he acutely appreciates the special nature of life in Quebec and is firmly convinced that its contributions to Canadian society should not go unnoticed or undervalued. Indeed, in speeches and interviews, he often shifts the rhetorical burden into the laps of Québécois separatists. It is *not*, he insists, that Quebec cannot realize its destiny as a nation while yoked expediently to the Canadian state, but rather that no vision of Canada as a modern society would be complete without the vital diversity that Quebec's presence in Confederation guarantees.

Quebec may flounder if it were to walk the road to independence, but the concept of Canada would be ruined, Trudeau thought. An advanced society premised on tolerance would have fallen apart as a result of shrewd appeals to a primitive tribalism. How, then, to avoid this outcome and integrate Quebec — special though it assuredly is — into a Canadian mainstream itself still being created? Discriminatory restraints on minorities could be lifted, Trudeau was confident, by the education and legislation initiated in the new push toward bilingualism and biculturalism across Canada. Albert Breton and coauthors, among them Trudeau, write:

The presence within a state of many ethnic groups poses problems of speech and culture which must be dealt with in their proper place. Let there be no doubt that we are against

23

the discrimination practiced by those who would have the English language as the only means of communication. But that is not to say that language should be a standard governing all politics. The future of a language depends upon the dynamism of those who speak it.

The last sentence in this excerpt from an early political manifesto suggests that it was another impediment that most exasperated the future prime minister: the tendency of Quebec's political leaders to scorn all that the expanding Canadian society had to offer. Throughout his life, Trudeau chafed at the implicit barriers placed before French Canadians by those who presumed vociferously to defend the "French fact" in North America. In the name of fidelity to language and homeland, generations of French Canadians were persuaded to consider themselves fortunate to be far removed from the chaotic worlds of technology, finance, administration, and statecraft.

To Trudeau, this celebration of exclusion was ruinous. The future, as seen by social thinkers from McLuhan to Marcuse, was bearing down quickly on the present. To decline to participate in it, to indulge the prevailing siege mentality, Trudeau realized, was not to stand safely apart from the encroachment of a cheap continental culture, but to hand over control of Quebec's end of the connection to distant, if not literally foreign, interests. Brian Shaw quotes Trudeau as saying, to the convention in 1968 that installed him as leader of the Liberal Party, "Masters in our own house we must be, but our house is the whole of Canada." And Trudeau writes in "The Meech Lake Accord," "the true opportunities of the future extend beyond the boundaries of Quebec, indeed beyond the boundaries of Canada itself."

It was as if his people, from whom he had never sought alienation but from whom at times he received condemnation, were being warned away from the twentieth century — not to mention the twenty-first. An irrational regard for tradition, which elevated self-handicapping to a ritual of cultural purification, is what Trudeau detected at the heart of Quebec nationalism, and he detested it with a passion that Canadian notions of propriety allow only to the French.

With time Trudeau must have compared himself to an ambitious son bucking the fatalism of parents whose sole accomplishment in life had come in transforming consistent defeat into a lurid badge of distinction. His love for these figurative parents and his respect for their years of suffering were manifest and real. So, independently, was his resolve to disobey them at every major opportunity. In defiance, he did not desire to be rid of the heavy weight of this family's history; he wished nothing so simple. Instead, he wanted to rewrite the family saga, in which lonely nobility is found in the pain of remembrance, into a story for the future. This story would not erase the past, but would transcend it. It would be a story not of vindication, but of justice; not triumph, but success; not victory, but peace. But to understand the story that Trudeau attempted throughout his life to write, we must first read the story that he sought to revise.

ONE SOLITUDE

The Quebec in which Pierre Trudeau was born in 1919 was one of the most insular regions on the continent, "the seat of North America's most stable and archaic rural society," as Everett Hughes puts it. Ron Graham, a political journalist, writes, "Certainly Quebec was still a claustrophobic, authoritarian, intimidated society heavy with incense and mothball patriotism when Trudeau was growing up in the 1920s and 1930s. . . ." Not all of its territory was remote or unpopulated; indeed, the fertile strip along the shores of the St. Lawrence River lies only a short distance from the American border and contains some of the oldest settlements in the New World.

Yet, like the old walled city that was and is its capital, the culture of the province was a sort of fortress, repelling outsiders and keeping those enclosed within it safe. Outsiders included not just people from the United States, but English-speaking Canadians, Protestants, industrialists, and urbanites: persons metropolitan and cosmopolitan. Safety thus meant freedom from the disruptive influences that these strangers surely carried with them. It meant freedom for Quebeckers to be French and Catholic, close to their language, the land, and God.

Rarely has this vigilance in behalf of the venerable been captured more vividly than in Hugh MacLennan's *Two Solitudes*, a moving story of fearless love and tragic misunderstanding among several generations of English and French Canadians. The first part of the novel is set during the First World War, in a rural Quebec parish, Saint-Marc-des-Erables. Its priest, the rigid and domineering Father Beaubien, surveys his newly constructed church and reflects on his hopes for his people:

> the priest visioned the whole of French Canada as a seed-bed for God, a seminary of French parishes speaking the plain old French of their Norman forefathers, continuing the battle of the Counter-Reformation. Everyone in the parish knew the name of every father and grandfather and uncle and cousin and sister and brother and aunt, remembered the few who had married into neighbouring parishes, and the many young men and women who had married the Church itself. Let the rest of the world murder itself through war, cheat itself in business, destroy its peace with new inventions and the frantic American rush after money. Quebec remembered God and her own soul, and these were all she needed.

We can, of course, admire what Trudeau later terms, in "The Province of Quebec," "the cozy myth of our providential mission." It bespeaks in French Canadians a pride of place and peoplehood that is so modest and otherworldly in its aspirations as hardly to suggest arrogance or the possibility of abuse. In its fresh form, it is the ideology of simple and virtuous people who wanted to live in piety and peace beyond the fray that they feared had become the daily existence of common people in North America. Even the great Canadian nationalist Henri Bourassa was not immune to the temptations of this theory. "Providence has willed," Thérèse Casgrain quotes him as saying, "that there should be in America a separate corner where social, religious, and political conditions most nearly approach those that the Church teaches us are the most desirable conditions for society."

Nevertheless, this ideology periodically exposed a dark side to public view: anti-intellectualism, ethnic and religious bigotry, and idealized if not puritanical social conventions. And faithfulness to these patterns measured one's commitment to Quebec. If Quebec was a special place by reason of its religious and racial homogeneity, then were not members of other social groups suspect and, as a matter of routine, to be shunned? If Quebec remained humbly obedient to Christ and his church while France slid easily into decadence and secularism, then was it not because Quebec had bound its sons and daughters to a hard earth and a harder heaven? Was not all this sufficient admonition, then, to avoid modern attractions, which, as they were pitched to educated and urban sensibilities, threatened to corrupt Quebec's culture as they had its motherland's?

Was there any argument at all that favoured involvement of noble *canadiens* with *les anglais* and a world that was deaf to the rhythms that would regulate French Canada forever? "Why do it?" one could ask. Why hasten to imitate the cold, the stiffness, and, yes, the decay, that when discerned in English Canadians reminded one of nothing so much as death itself? The people of Quebec had died many deaths already; there was little in the experience to recommend it, little that gained in the repetition except an overly long chronicle of defeat. As Trudeau writes in "The Province of Quebec,"

A people which had been defeated, occupied, decapitated, pushed out of commerce, driven from the cities, reduced little by little to a minority, and diminished in influence in a country which it had nonetheless discovered, explored, and colonized, could adopt few attitudes that would enable it to preserve its identity. This people devised a system of security, which became overdeveloped; as a result, they sometimes overvalued all those things that set them apart from others, and showed hostility to all change (even progress) coming from without.

That is why our nationalism, to oppose a surrounding world that was English-speaking, Protestant, democratic, materialistic, commercial, and later industrial, created a system of defence which put a premium on all the contrary forces: the French language, Catholicism, authoritarianism, idealism, rural life, and later the return to the land.

These values were powerfully reinforced by the most pervasive social institution in Quebec at that time, the Roman Catholic Church. "The Church," writes Conrad Black, "was the supreme conservatory of the French language and the greatest guarantor of social order, the font of almost all social and medical services." Priests, whom lay people saw as men of learning as well as agents of the Church, played vital roles in Quebec as community leaders, personal advisors, and interpreters of current events. In rural parts of the province, they practically ruled.

Two well-known anthropological studies of French-Canadian parishes in the 1930s and 1940s clearly illustrate the centrality of the priest, or curé, in the lives of ordinary Quebeckers. In the words of sociologist Everett Hughes, "The curé brings together the powerful sanctions of religion, as stated in the august doctrine of the church, and the crises and problems of everyday life." In particular, the priest bore total responsibility for the inner lives of his parishioners, and was obligated to stymie their thoughts when they appeared to be heading beyond the boundaries of unadorned devotion or the level of the priest's own training.

The hierarchical attitude of obedience to church authority is reflected in a letter issued by a Montreal bishop. William Chamberlin quotes his words: "Let everyone say: 'I listen to my curé;

the curé listens to the Bishop; the Bishop listens to the Pope; and the Pope listens to our Lord Jesus Christ.'" This chain of divine command can also be elaborated in the opposite direction. The *curé* at the parish church of St. Luc, in a growing town given the pseudonym "Cantonville," did precisely this in a typical homiletic warning to keep holy the Sabbath. "I am not discussing," Hughes reports the priest as declaring.

I am telling you, as your pastor and rightful moral leader and guide, the will of your Infallible Church. God reveals to His Church His will; and His rightful representative, the Pope, and your bishop, and finally we, your pastors, tell you. God's representatives know these moral questions better than you do; it is their rightful prerogative, and it is for you to listen.

Challenges to this authority were relatively infrequent, and usually handled without overt incident. In addition, "life in St. Denis" (as the other parish is dubbed in the second study by Horace Miner), "puts no value on intellectual and philosophic conversation. Such things are all right for priests and teachers, but for the *habitant* [the French name for Canadian farm folk] — his interests do not lie in this direction." If there was little curiosity about the mysteries of the human world, then there was even less about God and his ways: "With little theological interest, related problems are not very apt to arise. When they do present themselves, they are taken to the *curé* rather than discussed openly."

The stability of this situation is not surprising given the heavy socialization that rural parishioners received from the Church. The sermon at Sunday Mass in the church of St. Denis was the priest's prime opportunity to shape the opinions of his flock. "There is continual preaching against the threat of communism in Canada," the field report notes, though an objective observer must have regarded the prospects of a transplanted Bolshevism as pitiably small. The real target of criticism was sympathy for the Republican side fighting Franco in the Spanish Civil War.

"The communist is associated in the public mind with the blackest of deeds and motives. Ethnic pride and unity are fostered. Quebec for the French, not for the communists, Jews, and English, is the vein of discussion." And where do communists, Jews, and the English gather, waiting to seize the countryside from the honest *habitant*? The city, so "City ways are attacked, and disasters and catastrophes are pointed to as God's punishment for sin. Dancing, drinking, and superstition are attacked." This orientation does not accurately characterize all of Quebec's history since the conquest by the British. Nevertheless, over the last century it perpetuated a religious climate that corresponded to the prevailing accent in Quebec on authority: authority in the community in the Church, authority in the Church in the French-speaking priest, authority in the culture in the French language and associated traditions, and authority in French-Canadian society in politicians whose movements were guided or squelched less by the popular will than by the commands of the priests. Through this closed circuit surged a religion that, by today's standards, was doctrinaire and fixed, even smugly moralistic. Paradoxically Quebec's authoritarianism yielded along with its religion an everyday politics smooth and flexible in its corruption.

BAD RELIGION AND
WORSE POLITICS

Pierre Trudeau earned a wide reputation during the 1950s as a keen critic of politics in his home province. In 1958, as a young attorney, he published in English a highly charged essay identifying "Some Obstacles to Democracy in Quebec." "Historically," Trudeau asserts at the start of his analysis, "French Canadians have not really believed in democracy for themselves; and English Canadians have not really wanted it for others."

Democracy was not won for French Canadians in armed conflict or as the product of a protracted power struggle, he notes. They never actively pursued a participatory politics; they never thought it their right to claim such a system. Instead, they had this system imposed on them in the late eighteenth century after New France had fallen to the British military and had come under British rule. The French in Lower Canada never warmed to the arrival of democracy, which most tied to their memories of the aftermath of this defeat. All that the French valued had preceded this episode, Arthur Maheux points out; all of it had been gained under monarchs, not elected officeholders. Democracy did nothing *for* French Canadians, and its imposition seemingly threatened all that they had accomplished without it. Trudeau notes that "regardless of how liberal were the conqueror's political institutions," the new subjects of the British crown "had not desired them, never learned to use them, and . . . finally only accepted them as a means of loosening the conqueror's grip."

Democracy was thus a foreign idea, and until recently Quebeckers treated it with the unveiled — if often futile — contempt that colonized peoples reserve for the cultural conceits of their oppressors. "And as was natural with a vanquished people," Trudeau explains, the French in what had become British North America "valued their new form of government less for its intrinsic value than as a means to their racial and religious survival." The French consistently applied liberal political tools toward absolutist social ends, or so Trudeau contends.

Others have argued that constant features of French-Canadian culture had also inhibited the growth of democratic sentiment in Quebec. For example, the "classical course," an education given to most sons of the French élite, concentrates on the study of historical authors who expressed scepticism about democracy. In general, French-language textbooks praised the institutions of monarchy as an integral part of the golden age of French rule in North America.

The Catholic Church did not contradict this message. It urged a concern for at least a theoretical morality in the political arena. Morality, however, was thought to inhere in the characters of individual leaders, not in different systems of government.

Human appetites and passions needed to be controlled, the Church instructed, but one political system was not necessarily superior to another as long as both fostered virtuous citizens.

Although Trudeau did not explicitly reject these explanations for the lack of support for democracy in Quebec, he paid greater attention to the perpetual imbalance in power between Canada's two major linguistic factions. Even under the best circumstances, Great Britain's colonial domination of Canada ultimately checked, if not actually thwarted, the limited brand of democracy offered to French Canadians. ". . . English-speaking Canadians, rightly considering that self-government is the noblest way of regulating social relations among free men, proceeded to claim its benefits for Canada," Trudeau admits, "but only after serving standing notice on the French that such benefits were not for members of a subject race." The rules of the game in Canada, which derived from Westminster, locked the French into a minority position, dictating that for them, as Maheux puts it, "The fruit of the democratic tree was indeed bitter and never candied."

The English had cynically arranged the parliamentary system to ensure their power. Realization of this, Trudeau suggests, must have led to disillusionment among forward-thinking French speakers who might otherwise have taken seriously the more heartening implications of representative government. The French responded by withholding moral endorsement from the system and by learning its rudiments so that, as Maheux points out, through defensive abuse of elementary principles, they might slow the entire works. Outwardly there was cooperation; underneath there existed, in the famous words of Lord Durham, "two nations warring in the bosom of a single state: . . . a struggle, not of principles, but of races."

Tactically if not philosophically democrats, Quebec's representatives in the early nineteenth century made the most of their status as national legislators. They and their voters would "rally for electoral battles or parliamentary debates whenever their ethnic survival seemed to be imperilled, as men in an army whose sole purpose is to drive the *Anglais* back." The problem with their legacy is that, "as everyone knows," according to Trudeau, a band whipped together by military discipline and motivated by the scent of a battle "is a poor training corps for democracy, no matter how inspiring its cause."

For decades in Canada, democracy barely limped along. It had been badly injured at the outset, Trudeau charges, by a conflict in which the prosecution of narrow ethnic antagonisms became the object of national politics. This habit eventually resulted in a situation wherein the French-speaking "one-third of the people hardly believe in" democracy, Trudeau estimates of his day, "and that because to no small extent the remaining two-thirds provide them with ample grounds for distrusting it." Somewhere in between these two tendencies, the commitment to the common good that democracy requires was lost.

In affixing much of the blame for an abiding neglect of the common good in Quebec on the residues of a persistent conflict between linguistic groups under colonial rule, Trudeau did not overlook the harm that the French had done to themselves. He faulted especially their zealous defence of the national religion, which embraced more than Catholic spirituality alone: it additionally justified the temporal authority that the Church in Quebec wielded with neither excuses nor shame. Trudeau further notes in "Some Obstacles" that "since the dividing line between the spiritual and the temporal may be very fine or even confused," defenders of the faith in French Canada were "often disinclined to seek truth in temporal affairs through the mere counting of heads." Thus the legitimacy of democracy was weakened, first by a reluctance to believe in higher things, and then by the uncritical acceptance of belief.

Under British domination, moreover, the Church became a repository for nationalist sentiment among francophones, Herbert Quinn points out, and it thereby competed with the state for the ultimate allegiance of citizens. State functionaries were not to be trusted because they were assumed to be rivals who pushed interests inimical to those of the Church and, by identification, all French-speaking people. "In the political field," Maheux writes, "all attempts against the Catholic religion, the French schools, the separate schools, and the French civil law were deeply resented, and still are." At best, it was judged, the Church and the state could arrive at a bargain: the Church could deal for the benign neglect of the secular authorities, if not their outright indulgence. And deal the Church did.

So much dealing went on, in fact, that eventually masses of citizens in Quebec looked upon government not as a contest of ideas or as the principled execution of political choices, but as one grand system of barter for public booty — a civic bazaar, so to speak. And just as Quebec bartered with the rest of Canada to keep the federal government (and behind it Great Britain) at arm's length, so did its citizens barter with the provincial government for what was really their birthright.

French Canadians of the eighteenth and nineteenth centuries traded to England acquiescence in its parliamentary system for legal provisions establishing ethnic and linguistic rights. In the first half of the twentieth century, the men of Quebec traded their blood in Flanders fields and on the Normandy beaches to the king for, among other things, the protection of religious privilege. Still later, in the 1950s, as Trudeau notes, another generation of Quebeckers traded votes for a school, hospital, or bridge. Quebec has always sold what it felt were inessential pieces of itself, such as the personal franchise, to maintain the rest — its families, homes, and churches — free from external control.

LE CHEF

No one in Quebec politics embodied this ethic of exchange more thoroughly than Maurice Duplessis. He was the leader of the Union nationale, Quebec's longest-ruling nationalist party, which governed from 1936 to 1960 (with a short lapse during the Second World War). A French-Canadian political boss, Duplessis as premier accumulated power to his office to secure, above anything else, Gérard Bergeron notes in "Les partis politique québécois," his own popularity. "In the name of nationalism and religion," recalls Gérard Pelletier (the famed journalist and diplomat) in *Years of Impatience*, "Duplessis inflicted upon us a twenty-year reign of lies, injustice and corruption, the systematic misuse of power, the sway of small minds and the triumph of stupidity." Furthermore, Stuart Keate, a prominent newspaper publisher, describes Duplessis as "one of the most ruthless, despotic personalities Canada has ever produced."

Keate's blunt but largely truthful assessment was ventured after Duplessis's death and from the relative safety of a post in British Columbia. Other potential critics in locations more proximate to the living Duplessis and the reach of his retaliation avoided condemning him in public. They opted, at minimum, for deference. Part of their capitulation involved referring to him by his all-purpose title, *Le chef* ("The Chief").

The title was apt: for decades nothing that the government of Quebec did or did not do escaped the notice of *Le chef*. In the process, friends of Duplessis and the Union nationale were aided far beyond any standard of entitlement. Adversaries, on the other hand, discovered every avenue of appeal to the government blocked. The favouritism that Duplessis and his cronies showed to their supporters often exceeded the outrageous.

The Union nationale operated a corrupt patronage system virtually without rival in North America. "The patronage system under Duplessis is justly famous," admits Conrad Black, a media magnate and sympathetic biographer of the premier; he adds, however, that it is also "perhaps unjustly infamous." Certainly Duplessis did not invent political corruption in Quebec. His predecessors in the Liberal government of Louis-Alexandre Taschereau had widely practised the art. And so have Duplessis's successors. By the time that *Le chef* took office, corruption was commonplace in Quebec — as well as elsewhere in Canada.

Nevertheless, as Black points out, Duplessis brought unparalleled skill and unabashed gusto to the task of reaping the spoils from an antiquated political system. "Government in these times was wildly partisan," he notes:

> Like gluttonously hungry children who had watched the preparation of a mountainous cake now left unguarded, the Union nationale deputation swarmed through the vast kitchen of the provincial government. At first, they advanced timidly. Soon glee replaced respectfulness, intoxication banished continence, and what followed, while never approaching the decadent hauteur achieved in the December of the Taschereau regime, was more fiscally generous and vested with an incomparable spirit of joy.

With unusually large sums of discretionary funds in their budgets and unhampered by a nearly neutered Civil Service Commission, Quinn points out, ministers under Duplessis easily created and filled bureaucratic and public-works jobs. But accepting a job did not necessarily obligate one to work, especially if one were a child. In one district before the 1952 election in Quebec, he notes, the provincial Department of Roads issued payroll cheques to employees as young as five. He also mentions that

> Another practice, quite common in the rural areas and small towns, was for the Roads Department to make a detour from the highway in order to pave the road and the walk leading right up to the doors of a church. This was only done, of course, in those towns and villages where the parish priest was co-operative and his parishioners voted "the right way." (In these tactics the party showed no religious discrimination. The Roads Department was just as ready to pave the road and walk leading up to a Protestant church, always provided that the congregation of that church was friendly towards the party.)

In other instances, contracts for supplies were awarded to businesses run by local officeholders or other influential citizens, with the expectation of an endorsement in return. Party workers would later shake down these businesses for campaign contributions. To the businessmen's advantage, the amount requested (or coerced) was often hidden in the inflated prices that the province had paid for their goods or services. By this method the Union nationale was able to finance itself indirectly out of the coffers of the government that it controlled. This activity, again, went on outside the normal channels for political fund-raising. "The party," Quinn claims, "never made a public appeal for funds, never took up a collection at a political meeting, had no revenue from membership fees or the sale of party literature, and yet was able to spend an estimated three to four million dollars in every election campaign."

In the days preceding provincial elections, the Union nationale distributed some of its cash in the form of gifts to voters and their families. Alcohol, however, was the party's (and apparently the voters') preferred gratuity. "Thanks to the Union nationale," Quinn quips, "no one needed to go thirsty during a Quebec election campaign." Moreover, if a person had drunk so much as to trigger serious losses of memory, the party stepped in helpfully to furnish him or her with a new, if temporary, identity — perhaps one relinquished by somebody recently deceased. The forgetful but grateful individual was then escorted to a second or third polling place, there to cast another ballot for (of course) the Union nationale's candidate.

But the party did not limit its electoral crimes to the fraudulent impersonations of voters. It was also charged, at numerous times and in various places, with tampering with registration lists; buying voting certificates; stealing blank ballots to mark in advance for the Union nationale; stuffing ballot boxes at gunpoint; and spoiling ballots for opponents or simply discarding boxes of ballots in districts suspected of being sympathetic to the opposition.

Duplessis was not content, furthermore, to confine his actions against adversaries to election campaigns. He made liberal use of Quebec's restrictive legal code to harass his apparent enemies. One favourite tool of *Le chef* was the infamous "Padlock Law," officially entitled "An Act Respecting Communistic Propaganda." One of the first pieces of legislation to be approved after the Union nationale came to power, the law got its informal name from the authority that it gave to the provincial attorney-general (Duplessis) to empty without notice and lock for a year premises in which meetings of sundry subversives were rumoured to have occurred.

Persons who disseminated "communistic" ideas in print could also be imprisoned for a year, with no possibility of appeal. Moreover, they had to initiate legal action to establish their innocence, thus reversing the normal burden of proof in criminal cases. In 1957, twenty years after the Padlock Law's enactment, the Supreme Court of Canada, in the case of *Switzman v. Elbling and Attorney-General of Quebec*, declared the law unconstitutional because it infringed on federal jurisdiction over criminal matters. F.R. Scott, political organizer and poet, McGill University law professor and civil libertarian, was counsel for the challengers in this case.

Canadian constitutional interpretation finally caught up with Duplessis, who lost another important challenge, *Saumur v. City of Quebec and Attorney-General of Quebec*, which involved government suppression of pamphleteering by a group of Jehovah's Witnesses. In a companion case, *Roncarelli v. Duplessis*, the Court sided with a Montreal restaurant owner whose liquor licence the province had revoked after he posted bail for several hundred jailed Witnesses. Relief for the plaintiff, Frank Roncarelli, was dispensed too late, however: the business was ruined, and its former proprietor had migrated to the United States.

"THE LAST RAMPART"

What enabled Duplessis to hold power in Quebec so firmly and for so long, aside from a complex system of payoffs and punishments, was, as Kenneth McRoberts and Dale Posgate suggest, his skill in manipulating the sincere desire of average French Canadians for recognition of their special role within Confederation. Voters trusted him to win for them some autonomy from legislative bulldozing by the government in Ottawa. Black quotes him as railing that "the Ottawa government wants to seize the last rampart that we have to maintain the identity of Quebec and the characteristics of the province and of our race."

But as an autonomist, Duplessis had to walk a thin line, here stoking the fires of nationalist pride in Quebec, there dousing any demonstration of preference for separation. True, he gave Quebec its own flag, distinguished by a large white cross (representing the Catholic Church) centred against a background of blue. White *fleurs-de-lis* anchor each corner, symbolizing the roots of the province's cultural lineage in pre-Revolutionary France. True, too, this innovation came more than fifteen years before Ottawa designated a distinctive counterpart, the maple-leaf flag, for all Canadians. But in this manner, Duplessis proved that Quebec did not have to be independent in order to be different from — if not better than — the rest of Canada. Things were in good hands when *Le chef* (and he alone) could mediate for *la belle province* against *les autres*. And by most accounts — particularly those that he circulated through newsmen on the take — he did so expertly.

According to Black, more than a superficial correspondence fused Duplessis's personal initiatives and the collective longings of the people whose culture he and his policies rose to defend. It was a mating: "The province was profoundly seduced," asserts Black. "To be cared for materially with the love and discipline of a father, for Duplessis was genuine in the first and efficient in the second, and to be spiritually instructed by the mighty and intricate Church of Rome, was the fulfillment of Quebec's secret aspirations."

In a conservative society marked by patriarchy, Duplessis, though a lifelong bachelor, adopted the conservative style of a patriarch: he defended family honour against insensitive neighbours; he preserved his household's considerable human assets

and protected them from depreciation by renouncing speculation in far-flung markets; and he alternately indulged and
abused his children. In return, he demanded their unwavering
adoration, and on crucial family occasions such as elections, he
expected their absolute approval. The disobedient were dealt
with harshly.

BLACK AND SHADES OF GREY

This highly critical view of Maurice Duplessis and his influence
on Quebec politics is widely diffused through surveys of the
province's history. But there is a paramount source for his-
toriographical dissent from negative images of the Union
nationale leader — the massive biography written by business
baron Conrad Black.

Yet while Black's life of Duplessis introduces some valuable
correctives into the overly dark picture of Le chef, it fails to
communicate the desperation of Quebeckers outside the circle
of the premier's patronage. From Black's treatment of the brutality and bloodshed stimulated by a virtually mediaeval pattern
of labour relations in Quebec; to his rationalization of the
outrage caused by a ministry of grafters with their faces forever
lowered into the public trough; to his diminution of the bar-
barous political harassment and religious persecution carried
out under Le chef's orders — a barrage of pardoning words
sandblasts the memory of Duplessis and his tawdry regime to a
kind of retroactive purity.

Black is intemperate with Duplessis's many critics, celebrates
even trivial honours conferred on the premier, and lauds official
behaviour that would have been demanded by common decency
alone. Black's unyielding sympathy for his subject produces an
uneasy defensiveness: his account is generous to the point of
abject apology.

For example, he contends that "The Union nationale labour
policies . . . were not without merit." Duplessis's government

was "sympathetic to the defenceless and unorganized workers," but not to the "self-aggrandizement and unnecessary disputatiousness" of union bosses. "In all of these views," Black further writes, "history has yet to prove Maurice Duplessis mistaken, and his performance for the worker . . . was far from miserly." This opinion is debatable. But in Black's conclusion that ". . . Duplessis's had been probably the most reform-minded government in the history of Quebec," for all his understanding of the labour laws enacted under Duplessis, he is unable to distinguish sometimes generous paternalism from genuine, universalistic reform.

Black likewise insists that patronage under the Duplessis administration was actually "social and practical," a well-organized mode of public compassion. The handouts and payoffs, like welfare expenditures, "operated chiefly to the benefit of the constituents." A job was a job, no matter how it was obtained; a contract was a contract, no matter how it was awarded. Although the system was, by Black's admission, "unsurpassably paternalistic," financial indiscretions were confined, he believes, to "comparatively trifling sums." Ordinarily the money went where it was supposed to go: toward the purchase of votes, a practice that Black carefully sets off from the buying of elections.

The Union nationale held power for five terms, according to Black, because Quebec functioned as a democracy, and the orderly if dishonest rule of Duplessis and company was what the voters freely and repeatedly chose. "The Duplessis government endured not because it suppressed democracy," he asserts, "but because it embodied it." But here he confuses radical attachment to the popular will with conventional democracy. The former is but a pale imitation of the latter, lacking some of democracy's necessary components. Seldom in the era of Duplessis, in fact, could there be detected governmental commitment to the public purpose, to the voluntary subordination of personal gain to a notion of the common good, or to the protection of individual rights in the face of the will of the state.

Indeed, it is precisely on the issue of civil liberties that Black's apology for Duplessis finally wears thin. Black appears to defend the odious Padlock Law, in part because the controversial legislation was originally passed as a "publicity stunt," and because it was, after all, used against "active and admitted" Communists — as if these dubious claims exonerated Duplessis of blame for its creation and application or justified a criminal penalty for political dissent.

But Black bends too far altogether in his attempt to explain away the premier's shameful and punitive harassment of a tiny religious body, the Jehovah's Witnesses. The Witnesses, Black reports, "distributed hate literature at street-corners," invaded Quebec neighbourhoods and assaulted listeners with amplified religious messages, and generally sought to "proselytize aggressively." They were "zealots" "persisting in petty illegalities" and (gasp!) "becoming a public nuisance." For these high crimes against the state, Duplessis waged what he courageously touted as "a war without mercy" against the Jehovah's Witnesses in his province.

Like all wars, this one took its toll on both victims and victors. In seven years, according to Black, the provincial authorities engaged in some 1,665 prosecutions of Jehovah's Witnesses. *Le chef*, in due course, branded the group's champion, Frank Roncarelli, as one "inciting to sedition, public disorder and disregard of municipal by-laws," all for daring to post bail for Witnesses imprisoned for evangelistic activity.

Duplessis's words thus stand as the clearest indication of his abuse of state power in this matter. "It was like hunting," Black notes of this persecution, then dismisses it with the observation that, to Duplessis, chasing Jehovah's Witnesses "was good sport." They were a "fanatical and practically inconsequential sect," argues Black, and though the campaign against them was not "a very edifying episode," neither, in his opinion, was it "quite the barbarity that his adversaries have presented to a drooling posterity."

Black declares emphatically that "the uninitiated of posterity" are wrong to believe that "dumb tenebrous primitivism" was the secret of *Le chef*'s success in office. We may, it seems, allocate credit for the achievements of the Duplessis administration to many objective political factors without generating much dispute. But it should be clear that "primitivism" was evident in the premier's behaviour as well.

TRUDEAU'S EARLY YEARS

The Trudeau family lived in Montreal, and Pierre grew to maturity there when Premier Maurice Duplessis was at the height of his power. Yet much of Trudeau's early life was removed from brute contact with *Le chef*'s brand of authoritarianism. Trudeau's family was wealthy, and affluence purchased for him an insulation from much that was daily reality for ordinary French Canadians.

"Growing up as he did, in circumstances conditioned by class and by his family's unique characteristics," Ann Charney remarks, "Trudeau has always been separated by a gulf of experience from the needs and feelings of ordinary people living ordinary lives." Because privilege exposed the young Trudeau to experiences uncommon for Quebec youth, it was possible for him eventually to think differently about his society and its problems. This exceptionalism infected Trudeau's personal style and thought. Indeed, many of his contemporaries complain that the adult Trudeau is harsh and severe, distant and aloof. "He is a suspended brain, not fed much by the spirit, detached and cold," Edith Iglauer quotes David Lewis, a parliamentary adversary, as saying.

Another member of Parliament, Ed Broadbent, who as leader of the New Democratic Party faced the prime minister countless times across the floor of the House of Commons, sees in Trudeau a true ideologue. "Both in content and mode of action," Broadbent wrote of his Liberal foe in 1970, "his mind is that which frequently results when an intelligent youth confronts the ideas of seventeenth-century English liberalism: its declared openness barely conceals an intolerant rigidity." Even a colleague, former Liberal minister Jack Pickersgill, could be critical on this score. "This Prime Minister," Christina McCall-Newman has him saying, "seems to think you can govern by geometry."

Yet Trudeau's personal detachment, which served him in his early encounters with the world, later permitted him to avoid the errors of previous generations of French-Canadian politicians. In the end, however, his detachment left him unable to speak in the language of any nationalism that did not have a rational and instrumental basis. Likewise, Trudeau's political philosophy equipped him superbly to be the chief executive of a fractious modern state, to handle with skill the tensions that his country's internal divisions always generated. But ironically his philosophical adherence to individualism may have precluded a lasting solution to Canada's problems, for it admitted neither the existence nor the appropriateness of symbols that would emotionally integrate the entire nation in spite of its divisions.

AN UNCOMMON YOUTH

Pierre Trudeau's father, Jean-Charles Emile "Charlie" Trudeau, was an entrepreneur who, at a young age, became a millionaire through a chain of service stations that he had started in Montreal. Trained as a lawyer, he branched out into commerce in 1921 when he founded the Automobile Owners Association (AOA). It was a starting and towing service that also offered its members discount gasoline and oil at selected stations. Business was good, and after about ten years at the head of the AOA, Trudeau sold the firm to Imperial Oil, Canada's largest oil company (though controlled from the United States by Esso). The sale price was more than one million dollars.

With the capital that this transaction produced, Charlie Trudeau entered into more venturesome deals. In addition to mining, real estate, and stock-market speculation, his investments included the development of a huge amusement park on the island of Montreal and part ownership of the Montreal Royals, a minor-league baseball team that later functioned as a principal farm club for the Brooklyn Dodgers. In 1935, with the Royals in Orlando for spring training, Charlie, at forty-seven, contracted pneumonia and died suddenly. A brief obituary, "J.C.E. Trudeau," was distributed in the United States by the Associated Press and made its way into the good, grey *New York Times*. It identified the deceased as "one of the outstanding business men of Montreal" and "an ardent sportsman." It also incorrectly gave his age at death as forty-five. His estate was valued at more than five million dollars.

In addition to allowing Charlie to indulge his interest in sports and organized leisure, the wealth that he accumulated over his relatively short career in business made possible a comfortable standard of living — in Charney's description, "an atmosphere of ease and refinement" — for his wife, Grace Elliott, and their three children: Suzette, Pierre, and Charles. The family was cosmopolitan in a number of respects. Grace's father had descended from Loyalist stock, Scots who settled first in America and then migrated to Canada after the Revolution. Her mother, however, was French-Canadian, and Grace spoke French. Conversations in the Trudeau household occurred in both English and French; no one, according to Richard Gwyn, made much of the distinction.

Similarly, though Charlie often raised money for Conservative candidates and causes, and though he counted among his friends from school the premier, Maurice Duplessis, he had little use for parochial versions of nationalism. He maintained extensive networks of contacts throughout Quebec and Canada, and with his family he travelled widely abroad.

Young Pierre was educated by Jesuit priests at the all-male Collège Jean-de-Brébeuf, a French classical school about a kilo-

FIGURE 4

*As a Montreal schoolboy: a portrait of Trudeau
taken in the late 1930s while he was a student
at the Jesuit Collège Jean-de-Brébeuf.*

metre from his family's Montreal home. It was the only school that he attended from twelve until, at twenty, he enrolled in the law curriculum at the Université de Montréal. At Jean-de-Brébeuf in 1936, the year following his father's death, Trudeau met a special teacher, Father Robert Bernier. Over three decades later, Trudeau remembered how strongly he was influenced by Bernier, a scholar of politics and philosophy who taught litera-ture, a French-speaking Canadian and native of Manitoba. Father Bernier remembered his students as well. Iglauer quotes him as saying years later, "these were the sons of bourgeois, and didn't have money troubles, so they could throw themselves into art and beauty."

Robert Bernier also taught a course in history that was uncom-mon in Quebec at the time. "I insisted not only on facts and dates but on thoughts," he tells Iglauer, who sought some clues about the formation of the priest's most famous pupil. What thoughts, precisely? He elaborates:

the importance of the democratic spirit and the idea of federalism as a way of having political unity and cultural differences in the same country — a pluralistic society, with a sense of the universal and a love of differences for them-selves, where outside all the differences of nation, religion, sex, color, and so on, a man is a man, and is respected as such. I think the boys got something out of it.

At least one boy, Pierre Trudeau, picked up this much and more, as Clarkson and McCall suggest. The fifty or so adoles-cents in Father Bernier's class, living amid what he confesses was "a typical modern French culture — oh, a very French atmos-phere," nevertheless read thinkers such as Locke and Jefferson. "Our little life," as Bernier calls it, "gave the boys respect for the rational, an instinctive repulsion against the rising Fascism and Nazism." These forms of intellect blinded to reason are kindred to those that the adult Trudeau would locate within movements for nationalism in Quebec.

DEMOCRATIC ANTI-NATIONALISM

Another author on the reading list was Lord Acton, whose famous essay on nationality taught lessons that Trudeau as a grown man would never disavow. Acton claimed that nationalism became a powerful force in European politics with the partition of Poland. "Thenceforward," he writes in "Nationality,"

> there was a nation demanding to be united in a State, — a soul, as it were, wandering in search of a body in which to begin life over again; and, for the first time, a cry was heard that the arrangement of States was unjust — that their limits were unnatural, and that a whole people was deprived of its rights to constitute an independent community.

Acton recognized that movements for political change in his day often drew great strength from the popular desire to embody national aspiration in the structure of a state. But he pointed out that these movements stood in opposition to older revolutionary strains in Europe, particularly to the democratic legacy of the French Revolution. "For true republicanism is the principle of self-government in the whole and in all the parts," he contends. "In an extensive country" such as America, self-government "can prevail only by the union of several independent communities in a single confederacy. . . ." Democracy, in other words, "must either sacrifice self-government to unity, or preserve it by federalism."

A government for which democracy is paramount could tolerate only "an abstract nationality" that was "independent of the political influence of history." This identity alone could apply, argues Acton, because one could be committed to popular sovereignty only through a self-conception that "sprang from the rejection of the two authorities, — of the State and of the past." In revolutionary France, for example, "descent was put in the place of tradition, and the French people were regarded as a physical product: an ethnological, not historic, unit." Democratic equality requires the impersonality of universalism, so it effaces history. By this route, the French nation "became not only an abstraction but a fiction." Furthermore, the will toward a pure nationhood that the French had demonstrated is ultimately destructive, Acton reasons, because

It overrules the rights and wishes of the inhabitants, absorbing their divergent interests in a fictitious unity; sacrifices their several inclinations and duties to the higher claim of nationality, and crushes all natural rights and all established liberties for the purpose of vindicating itself.

A better way, he claims, is the British system, wherein personal liberty is emphasized over national unity. Political coordination is achieved under this arrangement not by the imposition of state power in the name of the people but through a vigorous federal competition, in which interest groups are positioned strategically against one another. A diverse population, according to Acton, "arrests the action of the sovereign by the influence of a divided patriotism." Prefiguring the pluralist theories of cross-cutting cleavages fashionable among students of political democracy in the 1950s, Acton explains that

The presence of different nations under the same sovereignty is similar in its effect to the independence of the Church in the State. It provides against the servility which flourishes under the shadow of a single authority, by balancing interests, multiplying associations, and giving to the subject the restraint and support of a combined opinion. In the same way it promotes independence by forming definite groups of public opinion, and by affording a great source and centre of political sentiments, and of notions of duty not derived from the sovereign will. Liberty provokes diversity, and diversity preserves liberty by supplying the means of organisation.

Diversity protects the people from the overreach of a government made giddy by its perceptions of the national will. "The co-existence of several nations under the same State is a test, as well as the best security of its freedom. It is also one of the chief instruments of civilisation. . . . [It] is as necessary a condition of civilised life as the combination of men in society." Acton firmly disapproves of homogeneous political entities: "that a nationality should constitute a State," he argues, "is contrary to the nature of modern civilisation." Sentiment for the creation of such entities, accordingly, is "a retrograde step in history."

LESSONS IN AND OUT OF CLASS

Trudeau's efforts to gain an authentic education after law school (a period of instruction that in retrospect he dismisses as merely technical training) were as erratic as his early schooling was disciplined. Increasingly the immediacy of experience, not the explication or recitation of an account, fueled the young man's learning. And experiences, of course, are sometimes messy.

Trudeau graduated from the Université de Montréal in 1943, then spent a short time as a legal clerk and in practice with a Montreal law firm. In 1944, he entered the United States to study government and economics at Harvard University, where his contribution, according to a classmate whom Martin Sullivan quotes, amounted to piercing the "frightfully earnest" environment of the graduate school with "a nice ironic sense of humor." At the conclusion of the Second World War, Trudeau headed for Europe and the École libre des sciences politiques in Paris. He left the following year for the London School of Economics (LSE).

"As a student at Harvard and the LSE," note Clarkson and McCall, "Trudeau had absorbed so much from the English — their nineteenth-century liberalism and twentieth-century Fabianism, their attitude to public service, their cult of cool self-containment. . . ." Personally bored and physically deprived in the austerity of postwar Britain, Trudeau finally abandoned formal classwork and began an unguided around-the-world trek, ostensibly to gather data for a doctoral dissertation in political science.

AROUND THE WORLD

With no itinerary or heavy luggage, and with little money, Trudeau set out east across the Channel and over the Continent. Equipped with false identification, he crossed the zones of military occupation in Germany and moved through Austria to Hungary, where he earned a free trip to Poland by agreeing to act as an interpreter for communist students en route there for an international fair. In Poland, he hitched a ride on an Aeroflot plane to Yugoslavia, where he was promptly jailed because he lacked authorization to enter the country. Largely to rid themselves of him, officials in Belgrade granted Trudeau an exit visa and expelled him to Bulgaria. There the young traveller was protected by a band of Sephardic Jewish refugees, with whom he communicated in Spanish.

From Bulgaria, Trudeau wandered to Greece and Turkey, then into the Middle East. In Palestine, Arab soldiers arrested him on suspicion of spying for the Haganah, but they soon released him. Trudeau crossed the Persian Gulf, and encountering harsh conditions (but safely eluding mountain bandits), he reached Pakistan and the political disarray of partition. A side trip to Afghanistan followed, as did a spell travelling through India and visiting French-Canadian missionaries in that diverse country. Trudeau's travels extended to Burma (ravaged then by civil war), Thailand, Cambodia, and Indochina (where he was assisted by French troops in the field). He shipped out of Indochina to Hong Kong, which became his stepping-off point for a tour of China. Using documents from the Nationalist government, he was admitted in time to witness the final stages of the revolution.

After a year on the road and thousands of kilometres crossed in boats, by trains, and on foot — and with communist forces massing across the Yangtze River — Trudeau departed from

Shanghai by boat for Vancouver and home. At virtually every stop during his "research" trip, the graduate student saw at close range the stark human consequences of nations captured by the conflict of competing identities. He saw the dangerous condition of a world in which ideologies raged in wanton disregard for the interests of individuals. The destruction and suffering were like nothing back in Canada; their scale was not matched by anything in his previous experience. But some of the ideas in dispute — religious supremacy, ethnic solidarity, and regional autonomy — were all too familiar to be at all comfortable. Trudeau could not overlook these ideas in favour of raw images of the misery that they had wrought. Instead, he linked both sets of memories, and like a true son of Quebec, he forgot neither.

THE DEATH OF ILLUSION, THE BIRTH OF VISION

Pierre Trudeau's political ideas derive as much from scenes in his biography as from themes in his philosophy. An early and formative scene took place in 1949 at Asbestos, in the mining region of the Eastern Townships, between the St. Lawrence River and Canada's border with New England. There the young man of twenty-nine witnessed a violent battle between Maurice Duplessis's provincial police and labour leaders at work making a modern Quebec. No wonder the event made a deep impression: in Quinn's words, it possessed "all the appearances of a miniature civil war."

The Asbestos strike, according to one Trudeau biographer, George Radwanski, "began the psychological preparation of Quebec society for abrupt and belated entry into the twentieth century." The strike, he contends, was a "collision between illusion and reality."

The illusion, fostered by the provincial government of Maurice Duplessis and the hierarchy of the Catholic Church, was

that Quebec remained a rural, agrarian society whose survival depended on inward-looking nationalism and unques-
tioning deference to established authority, and in which
there was no room for militant unions or any other groups
working for social change. The reality was that the Quebec
of 1949 was already overwhelmingly urbanized and indus-
trialized. . . .

Indeed, according to the Canadian census, by 1941 only 25.2% of
Quebeckers still lived on farms, and not all of them were directly
involved in cultivation.

One particularly repressive feature of the long-lived Duplessis
regime was its staunch opposition to independent labour unions
in Quebec. "In fact," Conrad Black writes,

no organism was surer of earning Duplessis's suspicion than
an externally directed and stridently voiced labour movement. Here was everything that the traditional Duplessis
disliked: property and its attributes contested; a potential for
violence based on a foreign dialectic transported into the
province and nourished by appeals to class and cultural
antagonism; resultant disunity in the French-Canadian
house, lost production, crypto-communist sloganeering,
and defiance of established authority, especially his.

Still, some unions — particularly those that accepted the
guidance of the Catholic Church — did get a foothold in the
province. In mid-February 1949, five thousand union miners in
and around Asbestos and other locations repudiated their government and walked off the job at the American-owned Johns
Manville Company when contract negotiations failed. As Sullivan notes, the union's main demand was for a wage of one dollar
per hour, a raise of fifteen cents over the prevailing hourly rate.
    The miners' union was an affiliate of the Confédération des
travailleurs catholiques du Canada (abbreviated CTCC; in
English, the Canadian Catholic Conference of Labour), a body,
Quinn points out, that had enjoyed friendly relations with the

ruling party. But the union refused to wait out the impasse while its case was passed to the government's arbitrators, as the law required. The strike against the company thus began illegally. One of the most famous labour conflicts in Canadian history, it lasted nearly five months. In that time, it altered forever the traditional relationship between French-Canadian workers, their government, and the Catholic Church.

Trudeau's involvement with the Asbestos strike began in April 1949, after he had returned to Canada from his world travels. A close friend, Gérard Pelletier, was an investigative reporter for the Montreal newspaper *Le devoir*, which had generally been critical of the Duplessis regime. Pelletier had begun covering the activities of the strikers regularly, and Trudeau invited himself along on his friend's trips to Asbestos. On one such trip, the provincial police intercepted and searched their car. The police detained them for a time, then ordered them to be out of town in half an hour. The pair complied for only part of the day.

Trudeau decided to put his dormant legal and oratorical talents at the strikers' service. He met up with Jean Marchand, secretary-general of the CTCC, who took the young, shaggily bearded attorney to a strike meeting. Marchand asked Trudeau to address the miners on points of labour law in Quebec. As Marchand recollected, however, Trudeau's speech was no delicate French-Canadian discourse on authority and responsibility. To the contrary, he reportedly "ridiculed policemen by recounting the derogatory terms used to describe them in the various countries he had visited." The same account, as Radwanski renders it, reports that, as emotion mounted, Trudeau instructed the miners "simply and eloquently about justice, democracy, freedom, and their right to fight for their cause." Marchand had gotten from his guest speaker more rhetoric than he had bargained for. "Miners are not schoolchildren, you know," Sullivan quotes him as later observing,

and while students might steal pencils, the miners steal dynamite. They use it all day at work, and they are very familiar with it. Now, I had managed to defuse two or three cute little plots by the boys which would have blown up the mine manager and most of his staff. So you can imagine that when Trudeau urged physical resistance by the strikers, I got a little bit worried.

Calls for physical resistance notwithstanding, it was Duplessis who consistently escalated the conflict and provoked violence. Not long after the onset of the strike, the premier, Quinn notes, acting in response to the company (but against the wishes of the municipal council), sent more than one hundred provincial policemen to Asbestos "to maintain order." Largely idle and sometimes drunken, the police were withdrawn until spring, when the company attempted to run the mines using strikebreakers. At that point, the workers isolated the plant with a picket line and cut off the town from outside labourers by blocking the roads. The police answered these tactics with clouds of tear gas and a request for rifle-toting reinforcements.

Official ire rose further when policemen found out that strikers had attacked several of their number during the initial confrontation. After a magistrate read the Riot Act from the front door of the church, Le chef's commanders released his troopers on a rampage through the town. They arrested townspeople in large groups, imprisoned them for days without charges, and denied them access to lawyers. Some, even those who had not resisted the illegal arrests, Black points out, were beaten savagely.

On the Sunday before these incidents (1 May, or May Day), the Catholic archbishop of Montreal, Joseph Charbonneau, issued words of support for the workers from his pulpit. In addition, he announced organization of a collection of money for their benefit. By following the example of the struggling labour movement in Quebec and demonstrating solidarity with the strikers, he not only defied the premier but sundered an ancient and mutually comfortable tie, a "holy alliance" between church and state in the province. Charbonneau was ultimately recognized for his courageous fidelity to Catholic social doctrine by reassign-

FIGURE 5

*A legal advocate for workers: as a young labour
lawyer, Trudeau attends a meeting in April 1957 of the
Confédération des travailleurs catholiques du Canada (CTCC).
During a pause, he converses with the trade union
organization's president, Gérard Picard.*

ment (some would say exile) to the chaplaincy of a hospital across the continent in Victoria, British Columbia.

In July 1949, after 120 working days, much expense, and even some blood (not to mention the permanent rearrangement of French-Canadian social relations), the strike was settled through the mediation of another Catholic prelate, Archbishop Maurice Roy of Quebec City. The miners received a new contract granting them a wage increase of ten cents per hour — what the company had been offering from the start of the strike. Later, when the union pressed a damage suit against the province for police brutality, one of its *pro bono* lawyers was Pierre Trudeau.

The Asbestos strike set Trudeau's political course for life. Radwanski argues that nothing in Trudeau's wide experience acted more viscerally to convince him of the enormous changes underway in Quebec and the need for modern thinkers to lead its people toward democracy. Until that point, Trudeau's forays into the public sphere were unmistakably those of a gadfly. Through the strike, he had glimpsed Quebec's future, and beyond it the future of all Canada. He envisioned a modern, industrial society composed of many peoples, bound by a government whose rational administration practised social compassion as it guarded personal liberty.

Perhaps most importantly, Trudeau saw a role in this future for a new type of leader — neither the brutal chieftains to whom Quebec had grown accustomed nor the limp brokers of interests in Ottawa who had tried so strenuously to hold together a splintered nation. There was a place for someone different: the practitioner of a rational, functional, and sensible politics. Anything less would cheat the Canadian people; anything more might defeat the Canadian nation.

AN INNOCENT ABROAD

The details of this new political vision and a description of an ideal leader were not immediately forthcoming. Pierre Trudeau had not yet become actively involved in electoral campaigns, in some measure because he was seldom in Montreal long enough to attach himself to parties or political organizations. Instead, he spent much of the following decade composing and editing political essays while intermittently travelling throughout Canada and across the globe.

While others of his generation were building reform movements at home, a vagabond Trudeau engaged the issues in his homeland from points far away. Travelling was valuable to him not simply as sustenance for his creativity but sometimes as its venue. During a trip down the Mackenzie River in the Northwest Territories by canoe and tugboat, for example, Trudeau drafted his famous essay on democracy — or the lack thereof — in Quebec. On an earlier sojourn in Europe, he edited much of the material for *La grève de l'amiante* (*The Asbestos Strike*), his collection of studies of the 1949 labour conflict in the Eastern Townships.

Indeed, Trudeau hardly ventured anywhere in this period without a writing project in progress or at least in mind. But the future prime minister was no mere compiler of pleasant travelogues. To the contrary, his writing often had little to do with where he was, or with whom. Trudeau took to the road not primarily to meet the people of the world, but to encounter the person within himself. Like the wilderness expeditions that he praises in his lyrical sketch, "Exhaustion and Fulfilment: The Ascetic in a Canoe," travel in general "assumes the breaking of ties." However, "its purpose," according to the youthful Trudeau, "is not to destroy the past, but to lay a foundation for the future."

In part, Trudeau left home so readily in order to test himself; however, the significant challenge away from home was first to locate the object of this test. Of his self Trudeau was innocent so far — hence his attraction to the new and different. His continuing pursuit of "the discovery of unsuspected pleasures and places," as he writes in "Exhaustion," gave free rein to warring elements within his personality: the student of abstract philosophies versus the man of immediate action; the proponent of logic and limits versus the romantic seeker after beauty in its infinite guises; the disciplined empiricist versus the footloose adventurer. All were manifest alternately during his journeys.

Trudeau's self-image emerged more distinctly the less he could rely on an unspoken affinity with his surroundings. In any alien setting, be it crowded or desolate, he was both in the centre of his personal story and absolutely alone, and he took a fierce pride in that stance. Early in life, in "Exhaustion," he describes the pride of a trekker through nature in terms worthy of a latter-day Thoreau:

For it is a condition of such a trip that you entrust yourself, stripped of your worldly goods, to nature. Canoe and paddle, blanket and knife, salt pork and flour, fishing rod and rifle; that is about the extent of your wealth. To remove all the useless material baggage from a man's heritage is, at the same time, to free his mind from petty preoccupations, calculations and memories.

On the other hand, what fabulous and undeveloped mines are to be found in nature, friendship and oneself! The paddler has no choice but to draw everything from them. Later, forgetting that this habit was adopted under duress, he will be astonished to find so many resources within himself.

COLD-WAR WANDERER

Pierre Trudeau's habits as a traveller were as casual as his goals were serious. He frequently left on short notice and stayed away for extended lengths of time. He threw in with all manner of companions and followed no ordinary package-tour itineraries. Upon reaching his destination, he would promptly elude his hosts and guides, the better to seek and explore novel locales on his own. Typical of this pattern was his visit to the Soviet Union in March and April of 1952 as a member of the Canadian delegation to a conference of economists and trade-union leaders. Trudeau went to the meeting in Moscow as a journalist, having received press credentials from *Le devoir* in exchange for the promise of a series of articles when he returned.

The Canadian government unofficially discouraged travel to Stalin's Russia, but this warning did not deter Trudeau. Nor did the advertised conference program, condemning restrictions on trade between East and West and apologizing for communist-inspired labour movements around the world. In fact, by some reports, Trudeau did not bother much with the business of the gathering unless the sponsors had put out a free buffet for a particular session. David Somerville points out that Trudeau was offered the services of both an interpreter and driver, but "he perturbed his hosts somewhat when he asked instead for a map of Moscow and stated his preference for lone walks."

For weeks, the young Trudeau roamed the city, touring houses of worship, sitting in the spectators' gallery during trials, and attending Mass faithfully each Sunday. He sneaked away from the drone of official speeches more than once for performances of the Bolshoi ballet. Somerville also notes that a friend who accompanied Trudeau on the trip remembers him cheekily requesting the works of Trotsky in a Moscow library and complaining to the staff when the outlawed writings of Dostoyevsky were not available in the stacks. He was even so irreverent toward the symbols of the Soviet state as to pitch an occasional snowball at the socialist statuary in Red Square.

Nevertheless, Trudeau found time to engage in a discussion with a panel of Soviet economists at the Academy of Science, an encounter that one of the British participants summarized six months later in a brief note for an academic review. When the conference was over, Trudeau remained in the country for the rest of the month, visiting Ukraine, Crimea, and Georgia. Finally, according to his recollection, the Soviet authorities asked him to leave.

A seven-part account of Trudeau's impressions of the Soviet Union began running in *Le devoir* in June 1952. The Russian people, he informed the newspaper's readers, are "kind but sickeningly conventional." He allowed for their adherence to communism, however: "when the alternative to believing is dying," Somerville quotes him as writing, "it's not surprising to find that the majority are believers." Trudeau concluded that "the country is progressing tremendously." The main drawback to this positive scenario, however, was that "it's progressing exactly in the way the planners want it, not the way the citizens want it." In the distant Soviet Union no less than in his native Quebec, the mechanisms of democracy mattered to Trudeau. His reward for this commitment was denunciation as a Red sympathizer (or at least a dupe of the Russian Communists) by the clerical élite in Quebec before the year ended.

TO THE CHINESE MAINLAND

Almost a decade later, Trudeau faced similar reactions. In 1960, he fended off criticism when he accepted an invitation to visit the People's Republic of China with a contingent of influential French Canadians, including his friend, the Montreal publisher (and later Senator) Jacques Hébert. Yet he went anyway, stayed for approximately one month, and returned without having succumbed to the allure of communist propaganda. The following year he produced with Hébert an entertaining record of their journey, *Deux innocents en Chine rouge* (*Two Innocents in Red China*). The book is a jaunty diary, brimming with sly observations and dry wit delivered with comic pacing.

The pair had expected an adventure; what they saw they impart with tongues often planted firmly in cheeks. The group, "taking advantage of a meeting he wasn't at," elected Trudeau as its leader. However, their passage east was almost aborted in London, on the initial leg of the excursion, because the Chinese diplomat who conferred visas noticed from Trudeau's passport that he had once visited the Nationalist stronghold on Taiwan.

Apparently Trudeau the veteran traveller could not satisfy any enforcer of political purity, right or left. After a delay of several days, during which the Canadians occupied themselves with a binge of theatre-going, they were permitted to proceed.

Much of the delegation's time in China was crammed with heavily staged exposures to life in industrial plants and on communes, mind-numbing recitations of economic and social statistics, toast after tipsy toast to enduring friendship between the peoples of China and Canada, and interminable performances by Chinese cultural troupes. (Hébert and Trudeau report that "the 'patriotic' numbers were less enjoyed than the others. This restores our confidence in the good taste of the Chinese public.")

What made it bearable was that, true to earlier form, Trudeau refused to acquiesce in the plans of his handlers for the tour. When he reached his fill of what the Chinese were offering, he insisted — politely but firmly — on making his own statements, scheduling his own meetings, and eventually breaking from his guides one day at a time. "And decidedly, when we are trying to get to the heart of a matter," Trudeau and his coauthor confess, more from fatigue than irritation, "we don't like being preached at all the time"; "You can have them: the General Line, the leadership of the masses, the Great Leap Forward, and all." Nothing could have prepared the stiff and stoic Chinese Communists for the results.

Trudeau and his companions peppered their hosts with rapid-fire questions, some of which were serious, some ironic or sarcastic, and still others lighthearted. For example, a visit to a jail in Peking elicits a request for an enumeration of political prisoners. Inmates under a sentence of death, they are told, have a period of two years for "rehabilitating themselves and saving their lives." "One imagines," note Hébert and Trudeau, "that some 'reactionary leaders' become excellent Marxists in less than two years. . . ."

A stop at a commune raises a query about whether mothers would prefer to work solely at home, looking after their families. A tour of a factory prompts the visitors to wonder how "unsatisfactory" workers are dealt with. At a teaching hospital, an administrator advises the group that in addition to learning biological science, medical students spend one day per week studying the thoughts of Chairman Mao. "Is this useful in the care of the sick?" the slightly stunned Canadians inquire. "You would say that the Church is free in China?" they speculate aloud to a priest of the Patriotic (i.e., non-Roman) Catholic Church; he answers lamely in the affirmative.

"What do girls dream about in China?" they ask a young woman who lives in a dormitory near her job site. "Oh — about their work, naturally," is the reply. "The worst of it is," Hébert and Trudeau lament, "it seems to be true." As he had in Moscow, Trudeau entered a library in China purportedly seeking books that he knew would not be there: in this case, "the works of Jacques Hébert. You are sure to have them all." Staff members took him seriously; they immediately began thumbing through the catalogue to the holdings of foreign literature, card by card. Their search was fruitless, of course, and Trudeau finally persuaded the dutiful librarians to stop looking.

At each stage of their trip, the Canadians' attitude was a combination of respect and scepticism. They were not so much anti-communist as anti-dogmatic. Their distaste for disingenuousness and cant was evident everywhere, though it was sometimes wrapped in a sharp-edged humour.

TRUDEAU MAKES AN ESCAPE

After hours of variations on "Twenty Questions" (with a few pranks to boot), the delegation's guides understandably hoped that their charges from Canada would retire early in mute stupor. But Trudeau did not conform. He was given instead to what Jacques Hébert calls "nocturnal escapades." In Peking, on the night of the celebration of China's national holiday, an evening when Trudeau shook hands with the exalted Chou En-lai not once but twice, he made his most daring departure from formal supervision. Leaving the gate in Tiananmen square, he lost himself in the swelling crowd. "What happened after that we shall never know exactly," writes Hébert, "nor are we convinced that Trudeau remembers it clearly himself." What follows is a dreamlike sequence that led the brave escapee far off the beaten track:

> He took part in weird and frenzied dances, in impromptu skits, in delightful flirtations; he described exotic orchestras, costumes of the moon-people, strange friendships, and new scents; he told of jackets of (imitation) leather, dark tresses, inquisitive children, laughing adolescents, brotherly and joyful men. Then he spoke of a weariness that imperceptibly settled on the city along with the dust, no longer kicked up by millions of dancing feet; he spoke too of lights being extinguished, voices growing hoarse, dances that gradually lost their speed and groups that grew steadily smaller; of trucks filled with soldiers at the end of their leaves, of busloads of departing peasants, of small parties straggling along the streets, of light footsteps in deserted alleyways, of dark lanterns, of the end of the masquerade; and of a very long walk through a sleeping capital in the small hours of the morning.

In the end, this kind of experience — spontaneous contact with the quotidian as well as scripted rites with the lofty — Trudeau yearned for when visiting foreign places. With a few exceptions, he did not have much of it in communist China. "We could ask almost anything of our Chinese hosts," Trudeau and Hébert write, "and they actually refused us nothing — except to talk to a Chinese without a witness."

As for many people of his era, world travel for Trudeau was a broadening experience. But it had a deepening effect on his character as well. It furnished a raw education, though for the young Quebecker its importance did not stop there. Travel to him was more than a source from which to draw entertaining yarns that he might later embellish. It was more, too, than an exotic rock against which to hone his intellect and capacity to confront quickly shifting circumstances. It was experience here and now, to be met on its own terms and cultivated for its own sake. Travel to Trudeau meant solitude without loneliness, self-hood without self-absorption. Steadily it gave him a freedom that reentry into the sphere of the familiar never forced him to relinquish.

AN APPEAL WITHOUT APPEAL

Fragments of Trudeau's political thought appeared from time to time during the 1950s and early 1960s in essays for Montreal publications such as Cité libre and Vrai. His broadest vision was not codified and presented, however, until 1964, a year before he joined the Liberal Party and earned election to the House of Commons from a Montreal suburb. The event announcing this vision was the release, in French and English, of a document entitled "An Appeal for Realism in Politics." Although jointly authored, the "Appeal" displays a simplicity of argument and a rhetorical directness hard to associate with anyone but Pierre Trudeau.

It is brief: in English it runs for just five pages. Yet the "Appeal," which discusses dispassionately a broad range of issues in national economic and political life, was self-consciously intended to be a manifesto for reform-minded Canadians. And though its seven coauthors were French-speaking intellectuals (three social scientists, three lawyers, and a psychoanalyst), their words were meant to carry with effect across Canada: in Quebec via the bristling review Cité libre, of which Trudeau was a founder almost fourteen years before, and elsewhere in the pages of the Canadian Forum, a left-of-centre journal of opinion in English.

"Canada, to-day, is a country in search of a purpose," the "Appeal" states in the opening sentences of a blunt passage addressed "To Every Canadian." "Emphasis on regional interests and the absence of leadership from the central government risk the utter disintegration of the Federal State." In Quebec especially, Albert Breton and coauthors note, "Emotional cries often drown out the voice of reason, and racial appeals take the place of objective analyses of reality." In an improved Canadian policy, rational objectivity — and the realistic leadership that should follow from it — would be premised on a single value: "the importance of the individual, without regard to ethnic, geographic or religious accidents," for "The cornerstone of the social and political order must be the attributes men hold in common, not those that differentiate them."

These lines are more than a routine call for amity and understanding between peoples. Americans, after all, frequently heard such entreaties during the 1960s. Considered in its own time and place, political advocacy on behalf of the individual in Canada was primarily a broadside assault on the notion that the special history and composition of Quebec society qualified it for special status as a homeland within the country, and therefore for special treatment by other governments.

That a group of avowed federalists reiterated this position was not in itself noteworthy. However, what ought to be noticed in this "Appeal," now as then, is the philosophical rationale for resisting a possible weakening of the federal system in Canada. The reason, which the authors proclaim with almost disarming clarity, is that particularistic bases for group identification — traits such as religion and nationality — in a modern polity ought to be invested, they feel, with no more significance than any "accident."

INDIVIDUALISM AND THE CANADIAN STATE

Surely this attitude is correctly applicable to all but a few members of any population when those members are taken one by one: an individual, it is true, does not choose the others to whom blood, place, or history has tied him or her. But this much conceded, it is a longer step to the opinion that such ties, for all their arbitrariness, are at best meaningless, are additionally illegitimate, and are usually destructive of larger human projects such as a political federation. Indeed, it is not clear that one can easily surrender these sorts of identifications. "The story of my life," argues the philosopher Alasdair MacIntyre, "is always embedded in the story of those communities from which I derive my identity. I am born with a past; and to try to cut myself off from that past, in the individualist mode, is to deform my present relationships."

Trudeau and coauthors grant indirectly, and perhaps unintentionally, the necessity for some collective sentiment in a national society. In spite of their emphasis on individual rights, these "realists" insist that a modern state should join its citizens to one another and the national ideal by "the attributes men hold in common." But what are these "attributes," if a prior commitment to pluralism excludes reference to race, religion, or nationality? Are not alternative kinds of attachment equally nonobjective? Are they not also inspired by emotions directed ultimately to the "accidental" facts of a biography?

Is a trait such as one's first language not a better criterion of belonging than other indicators to which "realistic" governments usually look? Birth or residence within certain national boundaries, for example, is one customary indicator of citizenship. Yet this situation is often accidental. Why endow this life-datum with great meaning yet neglect so many others?

Clearly the authors of the manifesto mean to espouse a different and more practical standard by which to assess the validity of an identity. "We reject the idea of a 'national state' as obsolete," they say. Writing by himself, Trudeau goes further, describing the nation-state in "New Treason of the Intellectuals" as an "absurd" concept, and likening nationalism, in Brian Shaw's compilation, to an anachronism no more viable than the divine right of kings. Still, the "realists" encounter difficulties, as do others who pursue their line of thought. The problem lies first in their failure to demonstrate that their desired mode of politics, anchored in a moral and political philosophy of individualism, is more "realistic" than the traditional collective forms that they reject.

Another problem lies in their failure to animate adequately a moral and political philosophy of individualism. In comparison, nationalism (individualism's chief competitor for popular allegiance) is overwhelmingly powerful. Yet not everyone assumes, as does Trudeau, that this power is to be feared. According to Charles Taylor, a philosopher and onetime electoral opponent of Trudeau, the "resacralization of politics" evidenced in nationalism carries an "immense contemporary appeal." This "appeal," he further claims in *The Pattern of Politics*, has as its cause "a deep, human aspiration, which is so far from being evil that it plays a central role in our development as creative individuals." Indeed,

> As long as the nation is made of ultimate significance, then we are all in some way priests of its cult by being citizens or members of that nation. The idea is so simple, and the potential so electrifying that it is not surprising that the cult of nationalism can release vast stores of energy.

"But we gain nothing," he adds, "by condemning all its fruits indiscriminately." "Realists" are likely to be frustrated, then, when they try to replace the emotional attraction of group affiliation with some individualist conviction, if one of comparable power even exists.

"First, there is the juridical and geographical fact called Canada," Trudeau and company observe. "We do not attach to its existence any sacred or eternal meaning, but it is an historical fact." Trudeau, then, does not rise to defend the spirit of Canada against suffocation by ethnic or regional specificity. For him, Canada is not a spiritual matter. On the other hand, he and his colleagues acknowledge their necessary confinement as indi-

viduals within the brute fact of the state. This acknowledgement, however, poses a problem of its own.

Groups of people set out their boundaries by creating an
identity, or by laying claim to an existing one. But identities are
not maintenance-free. If groups are to persist, they must have
what constitutes them interpreted for them. They must, in other
words, sense their deepest feelings of self being given form in
the conduct of collective affairs. The language of individualism,
however, is by its nature and design wildly ill-suited to formulating identity, for to accomplish that goal one must speak of
history and destiny in ways that circumvent, if not obliterate,
the individual. One must speak, if not mythologically, then at
least sociologically.

This demand of nation-building has always bothered Trudeau
deeply, as do the liberties with the factual record that nationalists
sometimes take in the reconstruction of a glorious history for
their people. Trudeau is frequently the first to object that all
identities are in some measure fictitious. In voicing this assertion,
however, he says nothing that reflective persons of whatever
background do not already know, if only implicitly. Moreover,
he mistakenly imagines that this point alone discredits nationalist sentiments. Because identities mix fact and fiction freely, the
history that each national image imputes will not be exactly true.
It must, however, have the ring of truth, or an appeal so powerful, so seemingly right, that its literal truth or falsehood becomes
a secondary matter.

Under these circumstances, the object for nation-builders is
not to render life as everyone knows it, but to promote an
identity that, though not objective, is both plausible and
humane. In the end, this object calls forth the much-ridiculed
"vision thing." Almost any history is variegated enough to allow
its transformation through a shared identity into a national
vision. Unfortunately the impediment to the creation of a plausible national identity for Canada is not the substance of the
Canadian story but the technique for its interpretation. A clear
national identity cannot be shaped with an exclusive focus on the

individual as the sole agent of moral and legal consequence, and with a reading of history not as an allusive story but as a literal succession of facts. The poet and playwright Robin Mathews has observed this weakness. The Canadian identity has been stunted, he believes, because

> The liberal ideology teaches, invites, encourages the Canadian to think of himself or herself as responsible to self, to his or her own personal development. It teaches the Canadian to scorn history, to reject communal values unless they are the values of a fragmented, experimental, a-historical little ephemeral society of contemporaries.

Trudeau and cosigners of the "Appeal for Realism" understood a fundamental truth: in Canada, to examine the historical roots of the nation is ironically not to encourage its solidarity but to risk its division and possible dissolution. They therefore intended admirably to let rest the ethnic antagonisms buried like a harsh salt beneath the cultural topsoil of their diverse land. They attempted this delicate manoeuvre by holding out to Canadians an above-ground substitute for politics-by-roots: namely political guarantees of respect and protection as individuals. In principle, these guarantees should usher in the benefits of democracy and equality that the operation of an individualist ethic promises.

But it promises (or threatens) other developments as well. It removes individuals from the guidance of the group and the comfort of tradition. In addition, it forces on them a new identity as autonomous citizens. Because this identity sports in public the telltale marks of its derivation, it is both too recent and too contrived to be fully plausible. Moreover, its imposition disproves the strong supposition that a nation's past and future are historically determined. For this reason, political individualism compels people to realize that their collective fate is *not* fixed but open to what they will or will not do with it. "Canadians are not inhibited or directed by pressures of manifest destiny," Trudeau, for instance, claims in *Conversation with Canadians*. "Our destiny is what we choose to make it." Each condition, in turn, only exacerbates the need of the Canadian polity for a functioning and unifying myth.

The reforms that Trudeau and his supporters wished are part of a passage that modern democracies everywhere at some point traverse, usually with relief and even celebration. In the case of Canada, and especially that of Quebec, the defence of the individual was a break from the past, a liberation from a legacy of colonialism commanded from afar and political irresponsibility evident at home. "We must descend from the euphoria of all-embracing ideologies and come to grips with actual problems," Breton and company write.

But this preference is flawed, not because it exhibits a concern for the problems of individuals, nor because it shuns a decrepit tendency to evaluate them by their communal ties. Instead, the flaw is that this approach refuses to acknowledge that meaningful action presumes some ideological orientation, and that any ideology needs an anchor in the values of a community. The adoption of a group's values, furthermore, is not a contingent or accidental element of an individual's life; it is a prerequisite of moral action. MacIntyre writes convincingly of this necessity:

we all approach our own circumstances as bearers of a particular social identity. I am someone's son or daughter, someone else's cousin or uncle; I am a citizen of this or that city, a member of this or that guild or profession; I belong to this clan, that tribe, this nation. Hence what is good for me has to be the good for one who inhabits these roles. As such, I inherit from the past of my family, my city, my tribe, my nation, a variety of debts, inheritances, rightful expectations and obligations. These constitute the given of my life, my moral starting point. This is in part what gives my life its own moral particularity.

As politically welcome as a new emphasis on the rights of individuals may have been, crucial questions linger, and the hollow responses from Canadian reformers doom the plans of the "realists." If emotion in appeals for good civic behaviour is banished, then what motivation other than narrow self-interest remains to commit citizens to the preservation of individualism as a system? What account is left to shore up the plausibility of the synthetic identity that individualism requires? And where is direction to be found for the unending deliberation on the future that individualism makes inevitable? The liberal individualist position leaves these basic questions unanswered. In the end, the liberal eschews the task, thus replacing the hard work of nation-building with a blanket condemnation of the excesses of nationalistic fervour. But, as Charles Taylor wrote in 1970,

To condemn nationalism as such, for instance, as many liberals do (our present Prime Minister is one example), makes no more sense than the general condemnation of sex because of all the sexual perversions that we see in human life. Today the nation is one of the most important communities in relation to which men develop their sense of identity. That it should also sometimes be given the rank of ultimate reality, so that it overrides more fundamental values, does not alter this fact. And we do nothing to combat these perversions in just wishing that the whole thing did not exist. We can only fight such perversions effectively by understanding what underlies them.

The reliance of Trudeau's "realists" on "the attributes men hold in common" glows with the positive aura of communitarianism. But if their approach supports the prospect of a real national community for Canada, it is on a level so ethereal, so abstracted from common life and experience, as to be more a creature of intellectual debate than a recognizable ground for order. The "realists" try figuratively to cultivate the blossoms of national unity without digging into the soil to the roots. By not upsetting the surface, however, their plant is cramped. It may wither and die.

A QUIET REVOLUTION

The Quebec in which Pierre Trudeau and his coauthors drafted their appeal for political realism was a place far removed from the personal domain of *Le chef* Duplessis. Montreal still occupied the same location on the map, of course, but by 1964 a new Quebec had stirred. An old land was moving toward a new era. Although hastened by the writing and political agitation of Trudeau and others, this transition was more the culmination of an organic process than the achievement of particular actors. French Canadians refer to this process as *"la Révolution tranquille,"* or "The Quiet Revolution."

The opening phase of the Quiet Revolution is usually dated from 1960, the year that the provincial Liberals, headed by Jean Lesage, unseated the ruling Union nationale, which had broken down into disorder after the death of the autocratic Duplessis in 1959 and a quick succession of leaders thereafter. But the forces that produced the Liberal victory had been slowly transforming life in Quebec for much of the century.

The trends toward urbanization and industrialization that Trudeau had chronicled in his reflections on the background of the Asbestos strike were changing society in French Canada, eroding the people's defences against the outside world and redirecting their energies to a fruitful encounter with it. The Quiet Revolution was thus a revolution in perceptions. It was a change, William Coleman writes, "marked by the final rejection of the vision of Quebec as a society with a rural vocation, as a unanimously Catholic, defiantly spiritual entity." By 1960, the Liberal Party in Quebec stood poised to reap the political benefits of social and ideological changes.

A first step of the new government was to try to eradicate some of the official corruption that had been so pervasive under Duplessis. The rationalized economy of the new Quebec could not afford it, and the more sophisticated citizens would no longer tolerate it. Soon after taking office, Sullivan notes, the Liberal government sent telegrams to construction companies around the province, halting progress on all public works until the contracts could be reviewed. Investigators discovered numerous irregularities, and the government ultimately voided many of these agreements. The jobs were then put out for competitive bidding.

With the money that this move saved, the Lesage government increased public spending on infrastructure and endeavoured to develop the human capital of Quebec's citizens. The government reorganized the educational system and placed the civil service under the control of professional bureaucrats. Quiet though this revolution may have been, it was also sweeping. The time for change, which Trudeau had been predicting and urging for a dozen years, had finally arrived.

TO OTTAWA

Despite the successes of the government in Quebec City, the federal Liberal Party was not faring as well in this period. In the fall of 1965, the federal party, led by Prime Minister Lester Pearson, braced itself for its second electoral test in three years. The party badly needed strong candidates, notables whose ready-made followings would sweep them into parliamentary seats and give the Liberals a firmer grip on the national legislature. Recognizing this need, the prime minister went to meet with and, he hoped, recruit Jean Marchand, the Quebec labour leader.

Pearson had approached him in 1963 about running for a seat in the House of Commons, but Marchand refused the invitation in protest over a policy reversal that permitted the government to approve the stationing of American nuclear warheads on Canadian territory. Trudeau was so incensed that he accused the Liberal Party of "cowardice" and branded Pearson, a Nobel Peace Prize winner for his role in the resolution of the Suez crisis, "le défroqué de la paix" ("the defrocked priest of peace"). As if

FIGURE 6

*The wise men meet the press: Trudeau speaks to reporters
assembled in September 1965 to hear him, Gérard Pelletier,
and Jean Marchand announce their decisions to run as Liberal
candidates in the next federal election. Seated at Trudeau's
left is Marchand; standing at the rear is Maurice Sauvé.*

FIGURE 7

*The wise men converse: the trio (from left to right: Pelletier,
Marchand, and Trudeau) assembles later for conversation.*

that gesture were not enough, Trudeau announced that he would vote in the approaching federal election for a candidate of Canada's recently reorganized socialists, the New Democratic Party.

In 1965, Pearson, heading a weak minority government, again sought out Marchand. Would the famous Quebecker stand for election under the Liberal banner? Marchand agreed, but he attached one condition: the party would have to find slots as well for Gérard Pelletier and Pierre Trudeau, his two allies from the days of the Asbestos strike. Pelletier — by now a celebrated writer, editor, columnist, and television host — proved acceptable to Liberal leaders, but many of them balked at the demand that they invite Trudeau to run.

Trudeau had spent much of the 1950s and early 1960s on the fringes of legal practice, university teaching, and electoral politics. In the words of Bruce Hutchison, his was a "youth of authorship and agitation." "Throughout those ten years," observes his colleague Pelletier in *Years of Impatience*, "Trudeau could have described himself as being a committed outsider." He had been during that time, Walter Stewart quotes Marchand as once graciously saying, "underemployed." According to the historian Ramsay Cook in " 'I Never Thought,' " Trudeau was a man "whose wealth made permanent employment unnecessary and whose liberal views kept him out of regular academic life." Moreover, in political circles during the previous decade, Trudeau had acquired, deservedly or not, a reputation as an indecisive and whimsical (yet brilliant) activist.

In Canada, federal politics is highly centralized, and party loyalty is a lofty virtue. How could a loner such as Trudeau be adapted to this system? And where could someone like him be placed to ensure his election? The Liberals wanted Marchand, so out of necessity they scuttled their doubts about Trudeau and hunted for a riding so habitually and overwhelmingly Liberal that even the unconventional Trudeau could be elected by a safe margin. Finally they found it: Mount Royal, an anglophone and heavily Jewish area of metropolitan Montreal. Trudeau was parachuted down on the voters of Mount Royal in November 1965, and in due course he, Marchand, and Pelletier were presented with fresh tickets to Ottawa.

The trio was known in the capital as "the Three Wise Men" and in French Canada as *"les trois colombes"* ("the three doves"). The latter label was either a tribute to their role as messengers of reconciliation between the English and French populations of Canada or a less confident reference to their relative inexperience in federal politics. Both Marchand and Pelletier held cabinet portfolios in Ottawa. Marchand left the cabinet in 1976 and was eventually appointed to the Senate. He died in 1988 at sixty-nine. Pelletier later served as Canada's ambassador to France and in the United Nations.

A MODERNIZING MINISTER

Within months, Trudeau rose from the status of a backbencher to that of parliamentary secretary to the prime minister, the same Lester Pearson whom he had savaged in his political essays not three years before. Little more than a year later, Trudeau became the minister of justice when the incumbent retired.

As minister of justice, Trudeau embarked on a series of reforms that modified or repealed antiquated laws and fashioned anew Canadians' conceptions of civil liberties. Admittedly a strong advocate of the federal state, he nonetheless strived to limit its capacity to intervene in and regulate the lives of individuals. Governments, he had learned long ago, exist in order to protect and serve citizens — not the other way around. As he writes in *Approaches to Politics*,

> no government, no particular régime, has an absolute right to exist. This is not a matter of divine right, natural law, or social contract: a government is an organization whose job is to fulfil the needs of the men and women, grouped in

FIGURE 8

New ministers, April 1967: after elevation to the cabinet as minister of justice and attorney-general of Canada, Trudeau shares a joke with colleagues John Turner (centre) and Jean Chrétien (second from right). Prime Minister Lester Pearson is at Chrétien's left.

FIGURE 9

Already an MP, *but not yet* PM: *Trudeau jabs home a point in
an address at a conference of Liberals in Montreal, January 1968.
Five months later he would lead his party to electoral victory.*

society, who consent to obey it. Consequently the value of a government derives not from the promises it makes, from what it claims to be, or from what it alleges it is defending, but from what it achieves in practice. And it is for each citizen to judge of that.

This fundamentally democratic conviction has led Trudeau consistently to attempt demystification of state actions and promote the well-being of individuals as a legitimate end of state policy. He is no supporter of minimal government; he is not a libertarian or anarchist. He believes that citizens deserve many services from their government, and that it ought to have the power to secure these services for them. He is, however, a traditional liberal: freedom of the individual is to him all-important. Charles Bordeleau recounts Trudeau's speech to a Liberal party gathering in Ottawa in 1970:

The liberal philosophy sets the highest value on the freedom of the individual, by which we mean the total individual, the individual as a member of a society to which he is inextricably bound by his way of life, and by community of interest and culture. For a liberal, the individual represents an absolute personal value; the human person has a transcending social significance.

Sometimes a big government is necessary to guarantee services to citizens. But citizens, in Trudeau's philosophy, incur no obligation as recipients of these services to submit reverently to the government. With patriotism as with nearly everything else, he is a pragmatist: the actions of those trusted with public responsibilities resound more loudly than the anthems sung by those subject to these actions.

Trudeau's special initiatives as justice minister included an overhaul of Canadian law on divorce, which had allowed adultery as the only grounds for the dissolution of a marriage. Sullivan relates Trudeau's words to fellow members of the

FIGURE 10

*Seeking the nomination: Trudeau rises to acknowledge
the cheers and applause of his supporters at the April 1968
leadership convention of the Liberal Party in Ottawa.
"Trudeaumania" is reaching its zenith.*

House of Commons: "we are all here to legislate not our own personal morals upon the country but to seek solutions to evils which arise in a civil society and which must be solved by civil or criminal laws." He also won reform of Canadian criminal statutes pertaining to sexual acts between consenting adults. "The state has no place in the nation's bedroom," Richard Gwyn cites Trudeau as saying. According to Peter Newman, in *A Nation Divided*, Trudeau also said, "You may have to ask forgiveness for your sins from God, but not from the Minister of Justice."

ASSENT AND ASCENT

Trudeau's performance as a rational and pragmatic minister of justice entailed updating an archaic legal code at a time when all things practically cried out for the modernizing touch. What quickly followed this performance has been described widely, if not entirely accurately, as in Iglauer's article, as "a political accident." Prime Minister Pearson indicated in late 1967 that he intended to resign, and Jean Marchand declined an opportunity to run as his replacement as the leader of the Liberal Party. Because the party has followed an informal tradition of alternating between English- and French-speaking leaders, the search was on for a francophone politician experienced in the national government and, more than any other qualification, committed to maintaining the Canadian confederation.

Trudeau had introduced the legal reforms that he had resolved to accomplish. In addition, he had ably represented the federal government's position in opening negotiations with the premiers on reform of the Canadian constitution. A "Draft Trudeau" movement took shape, and the minister of justice eventually capitulated, though reportedly not until tossing a coin in order to make his decision. He was anointed the Liberal leader in a convention in April 1968, and two months later voters across Canada confirmed his decision by keeping the Liberals in power through victory in a federal election.

STRINGS OF CONTRADICTIONS

Reason, emotional reserve, and self-reliance: these are the signature traits of Pierre Trudeau's character. Yet the personality of the former prime minister is not composed of consistent strands of experience and reflection. Rather, Trudeau's personality combines strings of contradictions that, in conjunction with his well-known aversion to self-revelation and his preference for solitude, fairly frustrate attempts to understand the private man who is the source of so many public achievements.

Trudeau inherited great wealth but has practised austerity and asceticism to keep the potential for "enslavement to material things," as Arthur Johnson quotes him as saying, to a minimum. Although basically a loner, he has spent his life engaging the world, a man of abstract ideas plunging over and over into concrete political action. He possesses what Gerald Clark identifies as an "innate conservatism," yet his most important pursuits involve reconciling that disposition with a "demand for personal freedom." He is a man of avowedly Victorian style, a chivalrous suitor who nevertheless gained a reputation as a modern libertine. Deeply and conventionally religious, he constantly sought to empower average people to challenge tradition and propel society in a secular direction. He cares for his appearance with more than a touch of vanity, yet professes to be shy. He approaches his work with industry, vigour, and flair, but abhors a show-off. Certainly disciplined, he is a careful eater, parsimonious spender, and old-fashioned parent. Still, he is given to bursts of irreverent playfulness.

Trudeau is first and foremost *an individual*, with all the eccentricity that this tag implies. His psychological makeup is contrary by nature: he always seems to lean against the prevailing winds. Ann Charney notes that he prides himself on his self-control and willpower, which were stressed in his schooling. His highly developed inner resources yield a healthy self-confidence, but one that takes him in extremes to arrogance and rudeness. He suffers neither fools nor knaves. "When I look across the aisle from time to time . . . and observe the disdain with which the Prime Minister treats Parliament, and the way he looks at us in the Opposition," New Democrat David Lewis comments in Clark's article, "I often say to myself: There, but for the grace of Pierre Elliott Trudeau, sits God."

Coupled with a sharp mind, a faculty yoked solely to the most rarified of concepts, Trudeau's self-absorption accentuates his detachment from mundane human concerns. Consequently few common people grasp what drives him. "While mystery is always an essential part of leadership," scolds the journalist Bruce Hutchison in an open letter to Trudeau, "I suspect that, from design or shyness, you have overdone it. . . ." Indeed, he acts sometimes as if normal social expectations do not apply to him. After seeing Trudeau in the House of Commons wearing not wingtips but sandals, Prairie MP Tommy Douglas opined, as quoted in George Bain's "Canada Has a Case of Trudeaumania," that "It's going to be unusual to have a Prime Minister who has to struggle to wear store shoes."

From his time in school, set among scores of fellow students, Trudeau's behaviour, Ann Charney writes, was marked by "his withdrawal from intimate contact" and an "almost fanatical sense of privacy." These attributes were also manifest during his ill-fated marriage. For the most mature of spouses, they would have been severe irritants; for the woman whom Trudeau chose as his wife, they were insuperable.

Pierre Trudeau's thirteen-year marriage to Margaret Sinclair was a strange match from the start. The most striking difference between the two lovers, of course, was their ages. Margaret was only twenty-two at the time of the wedding; at fifty-one, Pierre was two years older than his new mother-in-law. More critical, though, was the degree of emotional preparation that each brought to so intimate a union. Neither, it seems, really knew what to expect from the other.

HEALTHY, SANE, NORMAL, AND OBEDIENT

Margaret Sinclair was born in 1948, the year that her future husband was making his way daringly across Europe and Asia in the aftermath of World War II. She was the fourth of five daughters of James Sinclair, a Liberal member of Parliament, and Kathleen Bernard Sinclair, a nurse.

Margaret describes her upbringing in Vancouver during the 1950s and '60s as mostly ordinary. She spent her childhood, she says in *Beyond Reason*, with "healthy, sane parents" and "four normal, obedient sisters." The Sinclair family was a political one, but it kept policy issues and domestic life largely separated. Although her father eventually rose to the federal cabinet as the minister of fisheries under Prime Minister Louis St. Laurent, Margaret confesses in Carol McLeod's *Wives of the Canadian Prime Ministers* that the family rarely discussed politics at home.

She derived from her early experiences two insecurities: from her parents on one side and her sisters on the other. Margaret was sharply at odds with the economical and unemotional — even puritanical — nature of her Scottish immigrant father ("the dour outlook of a Presbyterian Scot," she terms it in *Beyond Reason*), and uncomfortable with the occasional feeling of being overlooked near the tail end of a boisterous and competitive line of siblings. The neglected daughter fought these handicaps by cultivating the disapproval of authorities. In Margaret's own accounts of her youth, she appears as a selfish, insolent, and rebellious child.

But young Margaret Sinclair excelled in the classroom. After finishing high school, she announced that she was heading south for Berkeley, where both the University of California and a burgeoning counterculture awaited her free spirit. Her father objected to her plan, however, so she enrolled at Simon Fraser University in Burnaby, not far from the family home. There she studied English and sociology. Her father's opinions notwithstanding, she also experimented with illegal drugs and moved on the edges of radical campus politics.

PORTRAIT OF A BACHELOR

Pierre Trudeau had spent most of his adult years backing himself into permanent bachelorhood. "I've been a bachelor so long," Brian Shaw quotes him as conceding ruefully in 1966, "I don't remember why I decided to become one." In truth, Trudeau's endurance in the unmarried state may not have been the result of a conscious decision at all, because he certainly did not distance himself from desirable prospects. Attractive women continuously surrounded him. Throughout his various campaigns, legions of miniskirted students crowded hotel hallways and pressed up against airport fences for a glimpse of the man, a touch of his hand, maybe even a spontaneous kiss. Although political circumstances may have heightened their enthusiasm, their attraction to Trudeau was nothing new.

As a young adult, he was seldom seen without one in an ever-lengthening sequence of beautiful younger women on his arm. Indeed, those who did not know him well — including many members of the press once he entered politics — classified him as a playboy. Trudeau did not reject their characterization. Rather, he toyed with the perception that he was a happily carefree man of the sixties. He wore a leather coat; he drove a Mercedes sports car; he dated blondes.

But Trudeau's friends scoffed at the playboy label, for they knew him better. They knew, for starters, that he was no wild sybarite. Like the writer Heather Robertson, they knew that "His relationships with women had always been controlled and categorized. . . ." They knew, too, that his self-denial and guardedness with others likely meant that his social life had much the same frenetic yet ultimately noncommittal quality as his first forays into journalism and politics. ". . . Trudeau played the

Swinging Bachelor," observes Robertson, while "carefully concealing his rigorous Jesuit asceticism beneath a sly, sensual mask."

Still, he had remained unattached for a long time. Was he fearful that self-reliance would be the defining feature of his life, that he would be alone forever? Did he detect that, nearing fifty, "he was in danger of becoming everybody's bachelor uncle, a balding, slightly pathetic figure with soup stains on his trousers," as Robertson puts it? Was he afraid that, left to himself at the end, he would linger, in the words of playwright Linda Griffiths (with Paul Thompson), as "one of those grey-faced zombies that wander around Ottawa"?

MAGGIE MEETS PIERRE

The couple met around Christmas 1967 in — of all places — Tahiti. The Sinclairs had selected the Club Mediterranée resort on the island of Mooréa for a family holiday. Lodged there coincidentally was another Canadian fleeing the harsh winter at home: Pierre Trudeau, by now minister of justice in the Pearson cabinet. Earlier that month, the prime minister had indicated his intention to resign, and Trudeau sought refuge in the tropical Pacific in order to contemplate a run for the Liberal leadership.

Nineteen-year-old Margaret Sinclair first noticed Pierre Trudeau from a distance aboard a stationary raft while the politician water-skied in the bay. ". . . I followed his progress idly, more than a little impressed by the ease of his performance," she recalls in *Beyond Reason*. Later he stopped at the raft and started a conversation about (among other things) travel, student life, philosophy, and revolution. Margaret had no idea who her interlocutor was; her mother had to tell her. The Sinclair daughter knew him only as "Pierre someone or other." "He was shy, almost too shy . . . ," Margaret reflects. Although the two made a date to go deep-sea fishing the next day, she stood him up.

"Pierre struck me as very old and very square," she admits.

Aside from a chance encounter at the 1968 Liberal Party convention, more than a year passed before they saw one another again. In the meantime, Pierre Trudeau had become prime minister, and Margaret Sinclair had undertaken a foreign trek of her own to Morocco, then a magnet for North American hippies. But the unsanitary conditions — not to mention the rampant drug use and casual sex among her peers — repelled her, she notes in *Consequences*, so she returned to Vancouver.

A short time later Margaret landed a job in Ottawa as a sociologist with the federal Department of Manpower and Immigration, and she began to see more of Pierre. Their courtship was quiet and unpretentious: long, meandering talks about the issues of the day and clandestine dinners of spaghetti at 24 Sussex Drive, the official residence of the prime minister. Their closeness crept up on them until, one weekend at the prime minister's summer retreat along Harrington Lake, he got to the point. "Well, Margaret," Robertson quotes him as saying matter-of-factly, "perhaps we should talk about getting married?"

"I found her eyes extraordinarily beautiful," Trudeau recalls of his soulmate, a generation younger than he. More significant than physical attraction for Trudeau, however, was how his fiancée complemented his ascetic impulses. ". . . Margaret touched Pierre's repressed psyche," explains Heather Robertson. For Trudeau, the promise of a youthful flower child as his wife resuscitated "the sensual, irrational, impulsive aspects of his personality he had severely disciplined and denied since he was a child."

WEDDING STEALTH

Some practical obstacles had to be overcome before the wedding, and the couple attempted to keep the arrangements under wraps. Margaret went back to Vancouver, where she enrolled in

FIGURE II

In happier times: married only eighteen months, and with wife Margaret at his side, Trudeau is renominated as the Liberal candidate in his Mount Royal constituency, September 1972.

a language class at the Alliance française. She also began taking religious instruction to prepare for conversion to Roman Catholicism, the church of her husband-to-be. In each instance, Margaret told her teachers that she was engaged to a well-travelled lawyer from Montreal named "Pierre Mercier." Although the Catholic training that Margaret gained from a local parish priest was rudimentary to the point of caricature, she received tips on supplementary reading from her erudite fiancé, so she delved into Saint Augustine's *Confessions* and Cardinal Newman's *Apologia Pro Vita Sua.*

On 4 March 1971, Pierre Elliott Trudeau and Margaret Joan Sinclair were married in a private Roman Catholic ceremony in Vancouver. The small group of guests consisted mainly of family members, though a number from Trudeau's side were stranded in airports en route to the wedding when a major snowstorm hit eastern Canada. The couple honeymooned briefly at a ski resort in British Columbia before arriving in Ottawa on a wave of personal joy and congratulations from around the world.

HEARTH AND HOME
ON SUSSEX DRIVE

Yet all the positive emotion on earth may not have been enough to bring lasting harmony between two people so different at heart: the cerebral and brooding father figure, and the playfully erratic hippie girl. Pierre had at least anticipated the difficulties that Margaret would face as the youngest spouse of a Western head of government. One measure that he adopted from the outset, Robertson points out, was to place Margaret "off limits" to the media. But a bigger challenge for Margaret was Pierre himself. He was "extremely solitary by nature," Robertson quotes him as warning his mate.

Margaret soon learned how true was his description, and how lonely life could be at the centre of attention, alongside her "shy,

FIGURE 12

*A suburban father: before leaving for work, Trudeau
stops to talk with his sons Sacha (left), Michel (centre),
and Justin (right) in the driveway at 24 Sussex.*

unsociable man," as she deems him in *Beyond Reason*. Before long, Margaret was out of bounds not only to the press but to virtually everyone. Affairs at 24 Sussex were carefully regulated by its principal tenant, and no one — not even his wife — was permitted to interrupt the routine or intrude on scheduled events. As Margaret laments in *Beyond Reason*, "Pierre likes his life programed: the good, Christian philosopher-king who wants to live his life by his will, not by the vagaries of fortune." The cocoon of special intimacy that resulted from their isolation and secrecy, the pair proved, could smother as easily as it once had thrilled.

The breaks in this bleak tableau were few, but they were remarkable. On Christmas day 1971, nine and a half months after the surprise wedding, Margaret gave birth to a son, whom they named Justin. It was only the second time in Canadian history that a child was born to the wife of a prime minister in office. Suddenly young Margaret was again thrust into the spotlight, this time as a latter-day madonna for a country to emulate. More magical than this national nativity pageant was the birth, two years later and also on Christmas, of the Trudeaus' second child, a son named Sacha.

Each addition warmed Canadians' feelings toward the growing family at 24 Sussex while relations inside the old stone mansion soured. To make matters worse, the burdens of parenthood overwhelmed the inexperienced mother. Daily Margaret struggled with household personnel nominally at her service, and she felt abandoned by a busy husband who allocated time to her as if she were an importunate constituent. The couple quarrelled repeatedly over money and responsibility. Margaret Trudeau was, to put it mildly, an extremely unhappy woman — in her words, as quoted by Johnson, she was "very, very weary and very emotionally tight."

Margaret flailed around for something — anything — into which she could divert the energy that her anxiety had generated. Pierre was little help: his advice for his directionless wife was that she read the works of Plato. Instead, Margaret redecorated the house, bought new clothes, took trips away from the family, and joined her husband on the campaign trail. Yet her depression did not lift. It grew so intense, in fact, that in September 1974 she landed in the psychiatric unit of the Royal Victoria Hospital in Montreal, where she spent about two weeks for "rest and some tests."

Margaret's hospitalization ended shortly after it began, but her suffering persisted. Pierre desired nothing more than a stable home and a smiling spouse, "a companion to transform the gloom . . . and the solitude of his empty evenings," Margaret writes in *Consequences*. Confronted with her demanding behaviour, he was at wit's end; dealing with her outbursts, he was alternately tolerant and strict, sometimes indulgent and other times stern in his reactions to her misadventures. Neither response, unfortunately, much altered her downward spin.

In October 1975, the third Trudeau son, Michel, was born, but his parents were already well on their way to mutual alienation. ". . . Margaret and Pierre retreated into separate solitudes . . . ," notes Robertson. "Pierre became cold and distant," hardly a stretch for him; Margaret, in turn, took up photography, not a simple pursuit as she was more the target of the *paparazzi* than one of the professional pack.

"SEPARATE AND APART"

After exactly six years of married life, the couple agreed in 1977 to part for ninety days. Pierre stayed in Ottawa with the children and their nannies; Margaret skipped off to Toronto for a weekend in a hotel suite with the Rolling Stones, and then to New York City for acting classes. At the end of their trial period, they made it official. The Prime Minister's Office released a statement announcing that the two had agreed to live "separate and apart," with Pierre retaining custody of their sons.

"Overnight," Margaret observes in *Beyond Reason*, "Pierre became the most famous single father in the world. . . ." Indeed,

FIGURE 13

Remembrance Day, 1981: Justin (left), Michel (centre), and Sacha (right) look on while their father furnishes a whispered narration. To mark the occasion, a poppy replaces the familiar red rose in Pierre Trudeau's lapel. Over his right shoulder, Conservatives Joe Clark (left) and Erik Nielsen (right) confer.

FIGURE 14

The perennial athlete: Trudeau doffs his shoes and takes a turn on a trampoline set up as part of an outdoor observance of Canada Day in downtown Ottawa, July 1982.

throughout this upheaval, and amid the uncertainty during the months and years that followed, he earned enormous sympathy from Canadians for his devotion to his children and his humour in handling painful personal developments. For example, he corrected one news report that gave the Rolling Stones as Margaret's favourite musical group. Actually, revealed the prime minister, his estranged wife liked the Beatles better. "But I hope she doesn't start seeing the Beatles," Johnson quotes him as quipping.

The Trudeau marriage underwent its final rupture in November 1979, seven months after the publication of *Beyond Reason*, a tell-all chronicle of their life together that Margaret compiled with ghostwriter Caroline Moorehead. (A second and more sober book, *Consequences*, followed in 1982.) The break also came during the short-lived Conservative government of Joe Clark, a period in which Trudeau had been tossed out of office and into a spell of serious introspection (including a stint in Tibet) that the weight of power had not afforded him for over a decade. The couple did not divorce, however, until 1984. Shortly thereafter Margaret married Fried Kemper, an Ottawa real-estate developer. Pierre has remained unmarried.

AN ACTIVE AGENT

A fundamental trait defines Trudeau: how immovably committed he is to being the master of his life. In certain respects, of course, other people have influenced his thought and behaviour. The atmosphere in the home that his widowed mother Grace oversaw, for example, Ann Charney describes as being "very English, very civilized and very distant." This setting could only have supported his desire for mental space between himself and the rest of humanity. In a sense, however, Trudeau has *chosen* to allow events to influence him; he has been an active agent while his contemporaries have merely been victims of their circumstances.

"I believe that Pierre built himself consciously, and with great effort, into the kind of person he wanted to be," contends Pierre Vadeboncoeur, a consultant to trade unions and Trudeau's boyhood friend. Yet "Brilliant as he is," Vadeboncoeur says of his erstwhile chum in Charney's article, "he has had difficulty in relating to ideas that require other than intellectual perception."

TRUDEAU AS A CANADIAN FEDERALIST

In *Straight from the Heart*, Jean Chrétien tells a story made memorable — and comical — by Pierre Trudeau's utter seriousness about the integrity of the Canadian nation and his commitment to relying on reason to preserve it. The incident occurred at the height of debates concerning sovereignty for Quebec. Trudeau and Chrétien, his justice minister, were mapping strategy for the federalist side one day as they strode toward the Centre Block of the parliament buildings, where the prime minister maintains an office. Chrétien was voicing some second thoughts. Both men were French Canadians, yet they steadfastly opposed an initiative that the government of Quebec considered vital to French survival. Just as Trudeau, who was leading the way, slipped into the revolving door, Chrétien stopped. "Our position isn't logical, Pierre," he said. According to Chrétien, Trudeau "froze" for a second. The shocked leader then continued pushing the glass panel until he had whirled around and emerged back outside. "What did you say?" asked Trudeau.

Pierre Trudeau has written or spoken on the faults of nationalism and the virtues of federalism innumerable times and in numerous places. Indeed, we could rightly contend that Trudeau has built his entire political reputation around his views on these issues. But he is more than an antinationalist. "The Prime Minister's anti-nationalism is well known," writes the economist Abraham Rotstein in his 1969 article "The Search for Independence," "but not so apparent is the classical liberalism out of which this derives and how that shapes his basic outlook. A man of many sides claiming a pragmatic approach to politics, he is the most deeply ideological of Canadian prime ministers."

As the preceding story illustrates, Trudeau is first and most crucially committed — even overly committed — to reason. According to one of his biographers, George Radwanski, "Trudeau doesn't really acknowledge the individual's right to choose to be *irrational*, to put more weight on emotion or instinct than on intellect. He assumes that other minds function like his — and, indeed, have comparable intelligence — and shuns any other approach as a failure to meet the standard of acceptable behaviour."

Trudeau's insistence on rationality, however, goes so far at times as to resemble an ideology in itself. Indeed, his record in office and beyond suggests that he is willing to abandon, if not reason, then at least reasonableness when any of the first principles of his liberal credo are challenged. The economic nationalist thinker Rotstein notes this tendency well:

The cast of mind is unmistakeably that of classical liberalism. Despite the P.M.'s personal motto — *la raison avant la passion* — he himself expresses the triumph of ideological passion, not only over reason but over history as well. This stance is his personal privilege, but in the circumstances it is also the country's burden. No ideological determinism need be invoked to appreciate that his anti-nationalist obsession is part of a coherent and unshakeable philosophy of atomistic individualism. . . .

A RATIONAL FORM FOR THE STATE

Trudeau objects most strenuously to nationalism because he deems it an ideology of feeling, one that is therefore irrational. Despite his opportunities to amend his opinions on nationalism, rationalism, and identity, they remain remarkably consistent. His clear and logical philosophical framework can be distilled from a close reading of his essays on political topics, articles written across more than four decades. In these writings, say Clarkson and McCall, Trudeau

> turned federalism and its corollary, anti-nationalism, into fixed principles from which he would not budge. Federalism was to be his lodestar. Anti-nationalism was his new crusade. He would save his compatriots from the follies of the new nationalism just as he had helped save them from the repressions of the old.

I treat Trudeau's thinking in detail here because only through such a presentation can we know the appeals that Canada's main politician and leading citizen of the last several decades would permit as the proper substance of Canadian patriotism. Although others might give one or another point in this sequence greater emphasis, I state the skeleton of Trudeau's argument against nationalism and in favour of federalism as follows.

Nationalism is not a constant and everpresent force in human affairs. Rather, it is a relatively new development in history.

For most of human history, Trudeau contends in "Federalism, Nationalism, and Reason," nations — their populations and boundaries — were unchallenged facts of life, *"choses données"* or "just data." People had no role in choosing their rulers, and hence they could not manifest their will or satisfy their longings by effecting any particular political arrangement. The domains of nations were taken as fixed by superior powers, and individuals thought it neither necessary nor possible to change this situation. Territory was territory, and forces outside of, and distant from, normal social life dictated its extent. People were people, "the population came with the territory; and except in the unusual case of deportations, very little was to be done about it."

This situation changed, however, with the dissemination, during the seventeenth and eighteenth centuries, of the notion of popular sovereignty. "Since sovereignty belonged to the people" under this new notion, "it appeared to follow," according to Trudeau, "that any given body of people could at will transfer their allegiance from one existing state to another, or indeed to a completely new state of their own creation." He further argues that

henceforth it was to be the people who first defined themselves as a nation, who then declared which territory belonged to them as of right, and who finally proceeded to give their allegiance to a state of their own choosing or invention which would exercise authority over that nation and that territory.

This transfer of popular allegiance was to result from more than democratic self-government. It was, in addition, to culminate a collective march toward national self-determination. That is, new nations would be formed not only because politics made such changes possible but also because history *demanded* their creation. The nation-state was lent what Trudeau calls "an ethnic flavour," and the *national state* emerged.

States are made, not born.

"The . . . nation is not a biological reality," Trudeau points out in "New Treason of the Intellectuals" "— that is, a community that springs from the very nature of man." In modern times, the state has lost some of its previous taken-for-granted quality. Because the state is viewed, in the ideology of nationalism, as the outcome of a people arriving at self-consciousness, states could be dismantled or reorganized at will to fit the geographical dimensions and cultural contours of that people. "As each of the peoples of the world became conscious of its identity as a collectivity bound together by natural affinities," Trudeau writes in "Federalism," "it would define itself as a nation and govern itself as a state."

> *Conceptions of nationhood are based on will, not reason. They are "little more than a state of mind." Nations try to will themselves to statehood.*

What elements, at a given moment in history, determine which groups qualify as nations and which do not? Trudeau further declares that "the foundation of the nation is will." Thus, the peoples who ultimately succeed in occupying a separate and distinct space on the political map of the world are those who have expended their resources and energies "labouring, conspiring, blackmailing, warring, revolutionizing and generally willing their way towards statehood."

Nowhere, Trudeau adds, is there clear evidence of reason in this process. New boundaries are seldom more reasonable than those that they replace. "For all their anthropologists, linguists, geographers, and historians," he pointedly observes, "the nations of today cannot justify their frontiers with noticeably more rationality than the kings of two centuries ago; a greater reliance on general staffs rather than on princesses' dowries does not necessarily spell a triumph of reason."

> *Nations that are successful as states are vulnerable, ironically, to the claims that gave them rise.*

Because states are rigged together by various means, Trudeau argues, it is the rare state that is really as socially cohesive as its nationalistic ideology implies. What, then, prevents a disgruntled minority from speaking of itself as a nation, too, and pursuing the same solution to its problems that created the country in which it is subordinate?

Embedded in the theory of nationalism, as Trudeau points out in "Federalism," is the unspoken assumption that "every sociologically distinct group within the nation" possesses "a contingent right of secession." National states, he notes, therefore face "a terrible paradox: the principle of national self-determination which had justified their birth, could just as easily justify their death." It is possible to realize new nations in an old world if a nation is "a state of mind." But people often change their minds.

Therefore, "a mysterious process" of consensus-building must be undertaken to make the state appear natural and permanent. This "gum" or "new glue" of state consciousness is also nationalism.

To avoid such changes of the mind, the modern state, Trudeau insists, must cultivate consensus "as its very life." The burden for would-be nation-builders, as he was to be reminded while prime minister, is that "it is physically and intellectually difficult to persuade continually through reason alone." Once again, the most convenient substitute for reason, under these circumstances as at the start, is nationalism. It is just "too cheap and too powerful" to be overlooked or dismissed. Nationalism, Trudeau argues in "New Treason," is "the faith that takes the place of reason for those who are unable to find a basis for their convictions in history, or economics, or the constitution, or sociology."

Nationalism arises, then, from an irrational will to form a state not in existence, or to obey and thereby solidify one after its founding. Because nationalism is created as the unthinking handmaiden of the state, it too will pass when the preservation of the state and its "natural values" ceases to be important.

Nationalism is emotionally appealing because people want (and at some deep psychological level, need) to preserve and obey the larger authority that the "national will" has established. But this desire (or imperative) presumably will fade. Trudeau asserts in "Federalism" that "the nation first decides what the state should be; but then the state has to decide what the nation should remain." If such decisions are not authoritative, then the original creation will be seen as bogus (or at least incomplete), the nation's legitimating ideology will crumble, and the nation will collapse.

In the meantime, to promote nationalism without an awareness of the historical functions of nationalist ideology is dangerous. In theory, nationalism need not destroy rationality and freedom; in practice, it does.

Some well-intentioned political commentators have embraced nationalism, Trudeau reports: "they liken it to a dream which inspires the individual and motivates his actions, perhaps irrationally but not necessarily negatively." But he rejects this stance because it manages to "drain two centuries of history out of a definition." The historical record amply demonstrates to Trudeau the abusive nature of nationalistic ideologies. He instructs us in "New Treason" that "History is full of this, called variously chauvinism, racism, jingoism, and all manner of crusades, where right reasoning and thought are reduced to rudimentary proportions."

Moreover, "the moment the sovereign state was put at the service of the nation it was the nation that became sovereign — that is to say, beyond the law." In Quebec, for instance, Trudeau fears, in "Separatist Counter-Revolutionaries," "a public preparing to sacrifice all values — especially personal freedom and safety — to the idol of collectivity." And national collectivities, he scolds us in "New Treason," are customarily part of the "rubbish by which the strong justify their oppression of the weak."

Federalism replaces the drive toward national consensus on all matters with a habit, both rational and realistic, of compromise. A federal system thus reduces the need for nationalist emotion and the risks to individual liberty that accompany it.

Federalism offers governments a refuge from dogmatism as well as a civilized opportunity for compromise because it accepts the world as historically rendered and does not endeavour to transform it. In a federal system, different groups can live in dignity and with full recognition of their cultural uniqueness. They must, however, lay aside claims to exclusive control over mechanisms for national self-definition. In return, they can expect fair treatment from the government, for the federal state protects the liberty of all by respecting the supremacy of none.

A federal state makes no attempt to impose a national consensus when none is necessary or feasible; instead, Trudeau affirms in "Federalism," it "deliberately reduces the national consensus to the greatest common denominator between the various groups composing the nation." Federalism makes no demand on the higher precepts of those who live under it, except to ask that they abide by the terms of the social contract. Of course, that contract may change, and it ought to change if government is responsive to the popular will.

Thus is federalism especially compatible with the needs of liberal democracy in nations with diverse peoples. And so is democracy incompatible with nationalism. "A truly democratic government cannot be 'nationalist,' because it must pursue the good of all its citizens, without prejudice to ethnic origin," says Trudeau in "New Treason." "The democratic government, then, stands for and encourages good citizenship, never nationalism." Federalism, for its part, promotes democracy: "It is an attempt to find a rational compromise between the divergent interest-groups which history has thrown together; but it is a compromise based on the will of the people," Trudeau writes in "Federalism."

Canadian patriotism therefore consists in an ardent defence of the federal system and a rejection of claims to nationhood that would short-circuit its operation.

A country as heterogeneous as Canada can survive only as a federal state. The Fathers of Confederation understood this, so they drafted a charter striking in "its absence of principles, ideals, or other frills." To Trudeau's eyes, "the Canadian nation seems founded on the common sense of empirical politicians who had wanted to establish some law and order over a disjointed half-continent." This they did, in short, by using reason.

With greater historical accuracy, the Fathers of Confederation may be portrayed as *reasonable* if not *reasoning*. Historians agree that Canada's founders did what they could with what they had: they were, in the words of an old joke, "as Canadian as possible under the circumstances." Political scientist Philip Resnick describes the backdrop of Confederation more critically. The Fathers "did not speak the language of the Rights of Man or of life, liberty, and the pursuit of happiness," he complains. "It is hard to get excited about the handiwork of railway buccaneers and their kept lawyers." Pragmatic political accommodation may follow as a welcome byproduct of a federal system. Still, it is a far cry from the process of decision-making that Trudeau favours — rational deduction from shared premises for politics.

Rejection of nationalism is feasible only if something more attractive replaces it. This substitute can be a kind of federal nationalism, an elevation of the federal union to the emotional level of the nation.

According to Trudeau in "Federalism," "A national image must be created that will have such an appeal as to make any image of a separatist group unattractive." This national image could be composed in many ways. Some contributing factors would be concrete: examples are road, rail, and airline connections; extensive networks of communication; and safeguards against international economic dependency and exploitation. Other sources of national sentiment are cultural or symbolic: a flag, patriotic anthems, pledges, and the like.

But for Trudeau, the government should undertake these efforts primarily to incorporate the country's various parts more thoroughly into national life, *not* to create a national life that reflects the essential character of the nation. The latter option invites the hazard of igniting anew the flames of nationalism, and Trudeau states, in "Quebec and the Constitutional Problem," "I cannot believe that a pan-Canadian or pan-American form of nationalism would be any less prone to chauvinism than the French-Canadian form." "When I speak of Canada," Richard Gwyn quotes him as saying, "I do not have in mind an 'identity' which competes with that which a French-Canadian and a Quebecer, conscious of his or her specific history and roots, holds dear." He envisions no "higher-order Canadian 'personality' in which would be absorbed or subsumed" the cultural sentiments of the nation's many minority groups.

This option will fail, however, unless all groups and regions in a federal system are drawn fairly into participation in it, unless they all see that they have so valuable a stake in the system that they are reluctant to relinquish it.

Federal states, because they also require some version of nationalism to maintain themselves, are no more stable than other polities. Furthermore, federal systems sustain local cultures and respect regional loyalties. Hence, to offset the centrifugal pressures toward dissolution of the federal union, a country such as Canada, Trudeau writes in "Federalism," must "render what is logically defensible actually undesirable." It must, in other words, offer its constituent groups and regions tangible incentives to remain in the confederation. For as soon as the cost-benefit calculus shifts, the question of national unity is posed once more, and the absence for these groups of a more enduring connection to the country's future is especially glaring.

"The feeling of being a Canadian," Jean Chrétien, in "Bringing the Constitution Home," quotes Trudeau as telling the House of Commons in 1980, during the Quebec referendum campaign,

. . . must be based on a protection of the basic rights of the citizen, of an access by that citizen to a fair share of the abundance of wealth in this country and to the richness and diversity of its laws. . . . [I]f a person cannot feel that in any part of the country he or she will get a fair share, then they will transfer their loyalty from the whole to the particular part of the country in which they choose to live. . . .

Even if flawless, attempts to construct a new federal nationalism will see only limited results. For "in the last resort, the mainspring of federalism cannot be emotion, but must be reason."

Emotion cannot be entirely purged from political life, but Trudeau prefers in "Federalism" that it be "channelled into a less sterile direction than nationalism," which is at best "a rustic and clumsy tool" for national progress. History shows that nationalism, whatever its power to unify a mass by violating the liberties of individuals, ultimately destroys peace among nations and order within them. Trudeau is confident that "a people's consensus based on reason will supply the cohesive force that societies require." As for his Canada, ". . . I am suggesting," he concludes, "that cold, unemotional rationality can still save the ship."

CEREBRUM OVER CIRCUMSTANCES?

In the hands of a master rhetorician such as Pierre Trudeau, descriptions of constitutionalism and federalism fairly shine with republican purity. The necessarily impersonal fixtures of liberal democracy — the inviolability of conscience, the sanctity of individual freedom, and the dignity of governments installed by the exercise of the franchise — are lent in Trudeau's discourses a moral purpose high enough to promise their perpetual defence.

At this point, however, the power of liberal democratic rhetoric reaches its plateau, for in making individuals citizens of a state (as opposed to members of a people), and in seeing the state as a creature of its laws (and not a manifestation of an overarching will), democracies lacking a coordinated national vision neuter themselves. They may become so calculating that they sell short the futures of their own people. The threat, in essence, is that liberal democracies trade destiny for security, swap a standing in history for a standard of living.

Certainly a country could make worse bargains. But the danger in such a deal is that even the immediate political and material rewards gained by avoiding national ideology may slip away when citizens begin to question what, apart from self-concern, obliges them to remain in a land so reasonable, yet so seemingly without a reason. Fine precision in tending the affairs of state, after all, is wasted if the state can compose no more compelling a rationale for itself than that it is already in place and functioning smoothly. Governments often attempt to provide for the well-being of their citizens, but in a manner suggesting that both state action and individual welfare reflect larger imperatives that unite in common purpose the citizen and his or her government. This approach is impermissible, however, when a guiding theory outlaws concerns of the state that are larger or more abstract than the conditions of individuals.

WITHOUT VISION

This is the corner into which Trudeau's fidelity to liberal orthodoxy backs him. His sole escape is to imitate the American philosopher John Dewey and consecrate the symbols of democracy as the sacraments of a new civic cult. But the iconoclast in Trudeau resists even this option, which to him smacks of unreason, of a concession to a mass penchant for political idolatry. He thus claims the undisputed role of high priest in a cult with an exquisitely wrought theology, but one built from the barest fundamentals. His church of reason has no eschatology, no (God save us!) soteriology, no effective ecclesiology, little distinctive ritual, and few adherents. Unfortunately for him, the last fact follows directly from the others.

Trudeau has no room in his rational mind for the backwardness of his country's *ancien régime*. He has no stomach, either, for the revolutionary madness that gave France the guillotine and put bombs in Montreal mailboxes, as the militant separatists of the Front de libération du Québec (FLQ) did beginning in 1963. Democracy, and it alone, is his middle way. Trudeau is committed to it, and his commitment may be his most lasting contribution to Canadian politics. But a commitment to democracy does not erase the moral challenges of shaping a sense of nationhood for citizens under such a system.

This task is vital because democracy naturally inclines away from a positive vision for any people. As the distinguished American historian Arthur Schlesinger, Jr. wrote in 1949, the year that Trudeau returned to Canada from his voyage around the world,

democracy, by its nature, dissipates rather than concentrates its internal moral force. The thrust of the democratic faith is away from fanaticism; it is toward compromise, persuasion and consent in politics, toward tolerance and diversity in society. . . . Its love of variety discourages dogmatism, and its love of skepticism discourages hero-worship. In place of theology and ritual, of hierarchy and demonology, it sets up a belief in intellectual freedom and unrestricted inquiry. The advocate of free society defines himself by telling what he is against: what he is for turns out to be certain *means* and he leaves other people to charge the means with content.

Trudeau the democrat is a stirring figure. Yet he could never bring himself to explain, in other than consequential terms, why democracy serves well the mission of the Canadian government. By his reticence, he may in the end have failed the country that he worked so tirelessly to save.

THE STATE OF RATIONAL FORMS

The flat tone of rational rhetoric in a society without a national myth is distinctly heard in the speeches and public comments of Pierre Trudeau. He is especially eloquent. His achievements as a lawyer, essayist, and politician have relied substantially on his ability to marshal words in a cogent pattern and persuade others with their force. In this effort, however, he is doubly handicapped: as a man of reason, he will not permit his appeals to rest on other than rational grounds; and even if he were to invite his fellow citizens to a deeper appreciation of their nation, as a Canadian he lacks a legitimate set of evocative national symbols.

Thus, even with Trudeau's natural rhetorical talent, his arguments are always stunted, at least compared to debates in societies with active national myths. As moving as his beliefs in Canada and its people may be, the verbal energy in his speeches is routinely interrupted because he must invariably stop himself short of any mystically particularistic utterance — that is, any statement about the nature and future of Canada that rational observers could not understand or share in happy harmony. To Trudeau the orator, then, Canadian values are what any democratic polity would recognize as constituting good citizenship. These values include tolerance, respect for others, and the pragmatic support of liberty.

"I have some basic principles which I like to see applied in our country," Trudeau explained to an audience in Winnipeg in 1968, during his first campaign to become prime minister, "and they can be very roughly and easily defined in terms of liberty, a democratic form of government, a parliamentary system, respect of the individual, balance between federal and provincial governments, and so on. But beyond these ideals," he declares in *Conversation with Canadians*, "I am a pragmatist. . . ."

Trudeau's is a limited view of the first principles of political leadership, and it readily results in an identically limited sense of the symbolic weight of any governmental action. While his ideal government wields extensive powers, the meanings propounded

FIGURES 15/16

Defending the undefended border: although relations between
Canada and its closest neighbour during the early 1980s were
not smooth, Trudeau presses his cause with United States President
Ronald Reagan (above) and Vice President George Bush (right)
on separate strolls around the White House grounds, 1983.

in how it exercises these powers are exceedingly modest. "The role of the federal government then is to lend unity to Canada," Trudeau once told a meeting of his Liberal Party; however, he immediately diminishes the sacredness of this task by coupling it in his next phrases in *Conversation* with a pair of somewhat more mundane goals of government: "to act as supplier of national services" and "to offer economic stability to those regions which are less wealthy. . . . ."

The first challenge, preserving the unity of Canada, is as close to a spiritual quest as any that leaders in the profane circles of modern politics are likely to adopt; the latter two jobs, on the other hand, merely require feats of administration. That the man who was prime minister links all three in the same litany implies that he cannot discern this difference. Worse, as William Stahl points out in "Symbols of Canada," it may imply that to Trudeau *there is no difference*, that Canada's integrity is one more problem awaiting the application of a methodical government policy.

In an interview broadcast during Trudeau's 1970 visit to New Zealand, he placed a similar stress on government as a provider of physical comforts. He identified Canada as a country to be preserved because, as he claims in *Conversation*, it is "one of the countries in the world which has the greatest potential for creating a society in which quality of men's lives is foremost in government's minds." In "The Tempest Bursting," moreover, he insists that, for his government, "What counts is improving the life chances of every Canadian, not protecting the abstract rights of 'peoples.' " Such is the vision of the liberal technocrat who believes that public-policy decisions hinge on a rational calculus that any and all can perform with the same results.

Trudeau is equally keen to deflate higher expectations of the Canadian government in foreign affairs. ". . . I hope that we Canadians do not have an exaggerated view of our own importance," he said to the National Press Club in Washington, only about a year after taking over the helm of the Canadian ship of state. In the veritable mouth of the American behemoth, he damned his countrymen in Yankee eyes with the faintest of praise. "We prefer to think that our place in the world," he says in *Conversation*, "is such that we can occasionally experiment with good ideas without risking a complete upset of the whole international order." Canada can innovate, in his account, because it enjoys a position of relative irrelevance in the world arena.

If Canadians are to be relaxed at home and flexible abroad, then how are they to know in any given situation how to behave? What models for thought can be taken as authoritative, what modes of behaviour can be regarded as normative? The answer, as outlined by Trudeau, is vague. Canadians, he told fellow members of the House of Commons in 1969, "are participants in a land that is not a simple northern extension of a foreign state, not an historical accident, not a random collection of diverse persons, but a community of integrity, with its own dynamism, its own society and its own future." This view, quoted in *Conversation*, is of course negative definition. Insisting that one's country possesses distinctive features neither proves their existence nor exposes them to the scrutiny of others. It does not respond directly to the question of Canadian national identity.

CANADIAN CIVIC VIRTUES

Trudeau realizes this problem, so he often struggled to fill in the picture, if only partially. "We should never doubt that we are Canadians — that we are different," he warns in *Conversation*. Yet what makes Canadians "different"? Again, we can look to Trudeau's words for a tentative answer. One passage, excerpted from his address on cultural pluralism to a group of Ukrainian Canadians, deserves quotation here. Trudeau argues that Canada's multicultural composition,

and the moderation which it includes and encourages, [make] Canada a very special place.

It is a special place, and a stronger place as well. Each of the many fibres contributes its own qualities and Canada gains strength from the combination. We become less like others; we become less susceptible to cultural, social or political envelopment by others. We become less inclined — certainly less obliged — to think in terms of national grandeur; inclined not at all to assume a posture of aggressiveness, or ostentation, or might. Our image is of a land of people with many differences — but many contributions, many variations in view — but a single desire to live in harmony. We have concluded in Canada almost without debate that true greatness is not measured in terms of military might or economic aggrandisement. On a planet of finite size, the most desirable of all characteristics is the ability and desire to cohabit with persons of differing backgrounds, and to benefit from the opportunities which this offers.

To those who argue — as some still do — that cultural differences are divisive and weakening, that Canada would be less susceptible to internal dissension if we were all of the same mould, I respond with an emphatic denial. Uniformity is neither desirable nor possible in a country the size of Canada. We should not even be able to agree upon the kind of Canadian to choose as a model, let alone persuade most people to emulate it. There are surely few policies potentially more disastrous for Canada than to tell all Canadians that they must be alike. There is no such thing as a model or ideal Canadian. What could be more absurd than the concept of an "all-Canadian" boy or girl? A society which emphasizes uniformity is one which creates intolerance and hate. A society which eulogizes the average citizen is one which breeds mediocrity.

What the world should be seeking and what we in Canada must continue to cherish, are not concepts of uniformity but human values: compassion, love and understanding. Our standard in all activities should be one of excellence, but our routes to its achievement may be as numerous as there are Canadians who pursue it.

Canadians, according to Trudeau, should be united most profoundly by two related convictions: the uselessness and even danger of national uniformity, and the value of the tolerance that they extend — by principle, necessity, and habit — to the many differences that divide them. Typically Trudeau's Canada Day address to the nation in 1969, contained in *Conversation*, had tolerance, and how it distinguishes Canadians, as one of its themes. "It is the tolerance towards one another which forms such a basic part of the character of Canadians," he observed. "Tolerance and moderation are found in this country perhaps in larger measure than anywhere else; against them we can judge our stature as a country and as a people." An atmosphere of tolerance, indeed, "is the strength of Canada. This is the heritage of Canadians."

Two years later, Trudeau relayed a similar message to Canadians, as he did later that year to interviewers from a liberal church publication. Judging from Trudeau's statements, Canada's destiny is to build a society in which different people can live in comfort and peace. Canadians, moreover, will achieve this destiny through their brand of civic virtue: by tolerating others' traits, understanding other cultures, sympathizing with the weak, protecting the privacy of individuals and the openness of nature, using reason as the governing standard in public affairs, accommodating change, and adopting pragmatism in political choices.

THE CANADIAN THING TO DO

Canada's civic culture contains an array of public values that most countries in the West would envy. Yet the reason that many other nations could subscribe to the same goals is not that they are easy to attain, or that each aspirant could match Canada's accomplishments in making a humane home for a variety of people; far from it. Rather, there is no formal obstacle to appropriation of the Canadian value system because it contains nothing exclusively Canadian. No inconvenient history intrudes; no rigid chauvinism overpowers.

Indeed, most of the virtues on Trudeau's lists (tolerance, understanding, pragmatic accommodation, etc.) are sharply anti-dogmatic. They *do not* exhibit anything noticeably Canadian. By their nature they *cannot*, for once they become Canadian, they cease being virtuously inclusive. Under Trudeau's liberal individualism, humans are presumably bound by common standards of reason. Aspects of personal identity less expansive than one's humanity, in contrast, are deemed, in liberal theory, irrelevant to collective life.

As the basis for a potential national vision, the commandments of liberalism are fatally universalistic. Anyone may embrace them, and thankfully some nations do, and seriously so. But there is no reasoning offered for why *Canadians* are compelled to this choice, only assertion that it is the rational, nay, courteous thing to do. "Undoubtedly there are some broad values and beliefs held in common by most Canadians," the sociologist Ralph Matthews admits, "but most people throughout the world would profess similar ideals. They can hardly be considered distinctively Canadian."

CONSTITUTIONAL POLITICS

When the new Canadian constitution was signed in 1982, it was missing a crucial element: agreement to its terms by the government of Quebec. When the time came to commit Canadians to Pierre Trudeau's vision of a renewed confederation, nine of the ten premiers granted their consent. Where was Quebec? After protracted closed-door negotiations on the optimal distribution of powers between the federal and provincial levels of government, and after lengthy (if sometimes more public) comments on how to guarantee Quebec's cultural distinctiveness, its separatist leaders balked. Thus, the document meant to introduce a modern era of national unity in Canada became an unwelcome reminder of pernicious and tenacious division.

The Conservative who succeeded Trudeau as prime minister, Brian Mulroney, sought in the late spring of 1987 to rescue his declining political fortunes with a bold initiative in domestic diplomacy. Descending from the rarified heights of an electoral victory in 1984 to new lows in public trust after a series of scandals jolted his cabinet, Mulroney set his sights on a distant prize. He wanted to induce Quebec, his home province, to accept the Constitution. This prize had eluded Trudeau, a fellow Quebecker, and tainted the testy Liberal's greatest public hour.

THE MEECH LAKE ACCORD

To achieve this difficult end, Prime Minister Mulroney invited the premiers to Willson House, an official retreat at Meech Lake in Quebec. Among them was Robert Bourassa, Trudeau's longstanding adversary, whose provincial Liberal Party had swept the separatist Parti québécois (PQ) from power in Quebec City in 1985. Although a strong cultural nationalist, Bourassa had never in principle rejected the prospect of Quebec remaining within the Canadian federal system. Clearly there was the opportunity for a deal; the need was seen to be glaring, the various interests coincided, and the feeling of urgency was high. Brian Peckford, the premier of Newfoundland, described the situation somewhat ingenuously. Anthony Wilson-Smith and Michael Rose quote him as saying, "But once we got there, there was an extraordinary spirit. We just discovered we had an atmosphere where we really wanted to make a deal."

The first ministers gathered at Meech Lake on 30 April 1987. Ten hours of jockeying and trading followed, and to the astonishment of many political observers, they were sufficient to reach an agreement. Wilson-Smith and Rose called it a "potentially history-making decision" because it initially appeared that the first ministers were "prepared to alter the way in which some of the country's most important institutions operate." Bourassa's government pledged to sign the Constitution in the name of Quebec in return for the promise of an amendment to that document affirming the status of Quebec as "a distinct society" within Canada. Quebec also won formal recognition of its practice of reserving three of the nine seats on the Canadian Supreme Court for its judges.

But the other premiers did not go away empty-handed. Indeed, they quickly saw the advantage of being flexible in their stances on Quebec so that they might achieve substantial gains in intergovernmental rivalries that normally roost closer to home. Largely to compensate them for their acknowledgement that Quebec is not *une province comme les autres*, the others were ceded extra and unprecedented rights in relation to the federal government.

The new authority earmarked for the provinces was so extensive that some legal experts feared that the prevailing distribution of powers in Canada, arrived at with delicacy and recorded in the 1982 Constitution Act, would be upset forever. "We are not talking here about minor legislative amendments," wrote Marjorie Bowker, an Alberta judge, in *The Meech Lake Accord*, a widely circulated critique, "but rather about sweeping constitutional and political changes which will re-shape our nation for generations to come." Wilson-Smith and Rose quote one constitutional scholar, Stephen Scott of McGill University, as asserting that the Meech Lake accord "marks a major decentralization of power within an already decentralized state." Another academic, political scientist Robert Jackson of Carleton University, went further: "Canada is to become the most decentralized government on earth," Mary Janigan and coauthors quote him as predicting.

Under this revised constitution, provincial governments would possess the right to originate nominations for the federal judiciary and approve federal appointments to the Senate and Supreme Court. They would also share with the federal government the power to regulate immigration and control federal monies allocated to the provinces for social programs. Furthermore, Mulroney gave his word to the premiers at Meech Lake that he would soon entertain proposals for a thorough reform of the Senate to make that often inert body more representative of Canada's diverse regions. Finally, each province was accorded a veto over future constitutional reforms — a measure that Quebec alone had insisted on before, to guard its francophone culture from domination by federal dictates.

DEUX NATIONS DÉJÀ VU

The future of Quebec's French culture loomed as the most troublesome issue before the Meech Lake meeting. Fittingly, then, the designation of Quebec as "a distinct society" was later hailed as a "breakthrough." Premier Bourassa especially was pleased: the new constitutional accord "was a great step for Quebec and for all of Canada," he declared in Wilson-Smith's article; "now we will have a form of cultural security." Mulroney concurred, for he clearly saw that bringing Quebec into the Constitution was a significant event for Canada.

A nineteen-hour negotiating marathon ensued during a follow-up meeting in June, and at the end, Mulroney could boast of a new dispensation in the national self-conception. "Today, we close one chapter in Canadian history, and begin another," he announced, quoted in Herbert Denton's article "Canadians Amend Constitution." "Today, we welcome Quebec back to the Canadian constitutional family." The "distinct society" was no longer distinguished by its status as a symbolic holdout against the legal formalities of Canadian confederation.

Yet few analysts of the first ministers' pact, and not even all of its signatories, knew what that seemingly innocuous phrase referring to Quebec meant. (Indeed, the government of Quebec admitted as much in discussions over a year after the deadline for ratification had passed.) Most distressing in his vagueness — and apparent unconcern — was Bourassa himself. Flushed from the afterglow of the agreement, he took a wait-and-see attitude in a *Maclean's* interview with Wilson-Smith entitled " 'A Great Step for Quebec' ":

MACLEAN'S: *Do you consider this accord as bestowing a form of special status on Quebec?*
BOURASSA: I would not wish to engage in a debate of such concepts. But we can say that the distinct character of Quebec has now been recognized, and that in itself is very important for us.
MACLEAN'S: *Do you interpret the accord's reference to a "distinct society" as having particular legal significance?*
BOURASSA: It is possible that yes, it could have some such significance, although I cannot now specify what form that might take.

So the premier wished not to debate concepts such as "special status" for Quebec, even though he had convinced the federal government to add a provision like it to the Canadian constitution. Bourassa's reticence is not surprising: at this point, the definition of the term was, to him, inconsequential. What he had wanted was what he acquired: the rest of Canada's acquiescence in (if not capitulation to) a symbolic demonstration of Québécois resolve, a gesture partly designed to rob the PQ opposition of some of its avowed role as the true defender of Quebec's autonomy and destiny.

The danger in his otherwise understandable strategy arose in how others — particularly the Canadian courts — might interpret the characterization of Quebec as "a distinct society." Defenders of the accord argued that it neither bestowed new rights on any level of government nor redistributed existing powers. Rather, Meech Lake's proponents claimed, the recognition of Quebec as "a distinct society" was intended as a "rule of interpretation." As the Special Joint Committee of the Senate and the House of Commons *Report* points out, this description of the province would establish an "additional constitutional [value] that, when balanced with other values already represented in the Constitution, will be used to arrive at a fair and proper interpretation in the decision of a particular case." But the reality was more confused.

The historian Michael Bliss observes that "The Meech Lake debate was notable for a pathetically low level of discussion of the Accord's provisions in the context of the sweep of Canadian history." Indeed, when Bourassa was asked if he sensed having been involved in "*a historic agreement,*" he replied, in Wilson-Smith's " 'A Great Step' ": "I never think about history, only the present." If his statement can be taken literally and as a description of his habits, then it makes him an atypical Quebecker.

Yet, as however atypical a native of Quebec this answer cast Bourassa, it places him squarely in the mould of other Canadian politicians — to his and his country's detriment. To seal a deal on the nature of the Canadian nation without long reflection on its history indicated both a neglect of the past and an expedient, even arrogant, disregard for the future. Admittedly it is a rare leader who can predict the consequences of his or her actions. But it is a foolish one who makes no attempt to foresee them.

BLACKMAILERS, SNIVELLERS, AND A WEAKLING

Enter Pierre Trudeau. Within a month after the Meech Lake agreement was initialed, the former prime minister set aside his quiet practice of law in Montreal and shattered an extended, self-imposed silence on political affairs. Toward the end of May 1987, he entered the fray with a scathing denunciation, "The Meech Lake Accord," written in French, translated into English, and carried in newspapers in both Montreal and Toronto. Trudeau's response to the Meech Lake accord contained a familiar degree of unsettling invective, but it stated as well the solid themes that were, for almost twenty years, the premises of his actions in office.

The 1982 Constitution Act, and particularly its Charter of Rights and Freedoms, offered to Canadians, he notes in his article, the dream of "a new beginning for Canada, where everyone would be on an equal footing and where citizenship would finally be founded on a set of commonly shared values." Were such a condition to have been attained, it would have marked a stunning victory of reason over a fractious political history. Now, after the "balkanization" of Canada by a weird conjunction of federal spinelessness, Quebec paranoia, and provincial power-grabbing, "there is to be nothing left but tears."

Trudeau claims that the Constitution invigorated the Canadian state by restoring the edge in federal-provincial competition to the federal side. That the Constitution bound the provinces to Canada (and, not incidentally, vice-versa) gave the federal government, bereft of an indigenous founding charter and a ringing ideological legitimation, its lease on life. It meant that Ottawa "no longer had anything very urgent to seek from the provinces; it was they who had become the supplicants." This relationship — predicated on the expectation of "give and take among equals," says Trudeau — established "a creative equilibrium between the provinces and the central government," which in turn ensured that "the federation was set to last a thousand years."

Mulroney the negotiator destroyed all that, Trudeau charges. The incumbent prime minister, in his view, was "a weakling," and his handiwork "will render the Canadian state totally impotent." Mulroney had allowed Quebec's historical (some would say anachronistic) "siege mentality" to justify a wholesale reduction in the central government's powers. In this conspiracy, Quebec was aided by the other nine provinces. Trudeau explains how their grasping could be appreciated: "Inevitably, they had enrolled in the school of blackmail of which Quebec was the founder and top-ranking graduate." But Mulroney's failure to defend a vision of a united Canada from appeals against it could not be dismissed. Like Trudeau himself, "Those Canadians who fought for a single Canada, bilingual and multicultural, can say goodbye to their dream. . . ."

Trudeau's is a high national vision, albeit one weakened by its lack of transcendence and poorly defended by a political culture mired in the mundane. Nevertheless, to what interest, according to Trudeau, had this vision been lost? The defence of Quebec, a quest undertaken by people whom Trudeau brands as

> perpetual losers: they don't have the stature or the vision to dominate the Canadian stage, so they need a Quebec ghetto as their lair. If they didn't have the sacred rights to [sic] French Canadians to defend against the rest of the world, if we could count on the Charter and the courts for that, they would lose their reason for being. That is why they are once again making common cause with the nationalists to demand special status for Quebec.
>
> That bunch of snivellers should simply have been sent packing and been told to stop having tantrums like spoiled adolescents. But our current political leaders lack courage.

"But Trudeau understood what was happening," notes Robert Fulford in the national magazine *Saturday Night*. To describe the situation, he uses a characteristically Canadian metaphor: "The endless game between Ottawa and the provinces had been permanently changed by one side's abrupt decision to play without a goalie."

Trudeau later repeated many of his points, and with as few concessions to intellectual modesty, before a parliamentary committee that was hearing testimony on the proposed constitutional amendments. His warnings went unheeded, however, and on 26 October 1987 the House of Commons endorsed the accord by a vote of 242-16. The measure was supported by the three principal political parties represented in the Commons.

The package then went to the Senate, where Trudeau-era Liberals abounded. According to the Constitution, senators may delay passage of legislation for up to six months. In this case, the Senate consumed its half-year by holding hearings, at which Trudeau again testified. Senators also began formulating revisions to weaken the accord. But this action caused the measure to rebound to the Commons for a last, decisive vote. On 22 June 1988, the new constitutional agreement, in its unamended form, received the final approval of Parliament. Only seven members cast negative votes. The first year of a three-year clock had ticked away in an ominous countdown: the agreement had until 23 June 1990 to be approved by the legislature of each province.

MORE THAN THE
SUM OF ITS PARTS

Over the next year, most of the provinces assented to the accord. But as the deadline for unanimous passage of the constitutional changes negotiated at Meech Lake neared, the political situation grew more complex. In three provinces, new premiers had come to power, unseating signers of the 1987 agreement. Manitoba's Conservative party controlled just twenty-four of the fifty-seven seats in the Legislative Assembly, so it governed as a minority with the cooperation of the two opposition parties. In New Brunswick, the Liberals had glided back to power by capturing every seat in the legislature, and Liberals also rose to a majority in Newfoundland.

Neither Manitoba nor New Brunswick had ratified the Meech Lake accord, and it was now unlikely that either would. Frank McKenna, the new premier of New Brunswick, doubted that the provisions of the accord, if left unaltered, could adequately defend the rights of Native peoples and members of linguistic minorities across Canada. Although the premier of Manitoba, Gary Filmon, at first supported the accord, he was buffeted from the left by Gary Doer, leader of the provincial New Democratic Party, and Liberal leader Sharon Carstairs, who headed the official opposition. Both opposed specific elements of the accord. Especially adamant was Carstairs, who insisted that the 1987 pact "jeopardized the future of this nation of ours."

Too high a price had been paid, Carstairs protested, for the symbolic inclusion of Quebec under the federal constitution. The exclusive reference to Quebec in the "distinct society" clause of the accord denigrated the multiculturalism of Canada; the likely postponement of Senate reform ignored the alienation of the western provinces; the requirement of unanimity for the creation of new provinces deflected the aspirations of the northern territories; and the decentralization of federal spending powers threatened equality of opportunity for all Canadians. The terms of the agreement "made shivers run up and down my spine," she confessed. As an attempt at nation-building, the Meech Lake accord clearly "went backwards."

Eventually the outspoken Liberal's primary political adversary agreed with her. In December 1988, Premier Filmon withdrew his government's endorsement of the accord. He ordered this action after Quebec invoked the "notwithstanding" clause of the Canadian Charter of Rights and Freedoms to shield itself temporarily against a Supreme Court ruling that voided a controversial law banning the use of languages other than French on outdoor signs in that province.

With its new Liberal majority, the Newfoundland House of Assembly rescinded the province's approval of the Meech Lake accord. In the process, Premier Clyde Wells, a constitutional lawyer, gained prominence as the most consistent critic of the deal and, not incidentally, as an obvious heir to the political philosophy of Pierre Trudeau. To attack the accord was not to reject Quebec, Wells contended; indeed, such an assertion was "an offensive insult to the majority of Canadians." Rather, they, like Wells, were "rejecting the dismantling of federalism" that they spied beneath the surface of the text. In fact, the Meech Lake accord, in his opinion, was "seriously inconsistent with the fundamental constitutional precepts" of Canada. In a passage that Trudeau himself could have penned, Wells claimed that

> there is more to being a Canadian than being a resident of a particular province or territory. Canada has a national identity that is more than the sum of its parts; an identity which must be provided for and reinforced by the Constitution. Canada must not be allowed to degenerate into an association of provinces and territories known to the world as the "Canadian Economic Community."

As the deadline for ratification loomed, Trudeau launched a final assault on the accord. He folded it into the closing chapter of *Towards a Just Society*, a book that recounts the policy accomplishments of "The Trudeau Years." According to Trudeau the retrospective essayist, Canada in the not-long-gone days of the Meech Lake deal was saddled with

> a prime minister ready to trade Canada's soul for an electoral victory, and ten provincial premiers all panting to increase their powers by despoiling the Canadian state, with the backing of the small fry sitting on parliamentary Opposition benches who are terrified of incurring the disapproval of officially endorsed Quebec thinking.

In hopeful contrast, however, there also existed for Trudeau a "real country," for whose citizens ". . . Canada is a true nation, whose ideal is compassion and justice and whose desire is to be governed democratically in freedom and equality." Compassion and justice, freedom and equality: rhetorically at least, Trudeau's career had come full circle. But the nation's leaders had yet to choose between two images of their country.

At the last minute, the first ministers of Canada were summoned to the capital for a desperate round of largely back-room negotiations designed to pressure the holdout premiers, win their consent, and thereby avoid the deal's demise. The Ottawa talks, though strained by acrimony and plagued by repeated threats of walkouts, ground on nevertheless for seven days. "The negotiations themselves," notes Reg Whitaker, "were a kind of Monty Python hostage drama: the dissenting premiers kidnapped and held in Ottawa by nine desperate first ministers who insisted on their signatures before letting them go." A feeling of crisis overtook the discussions, and previously resolute wills weakened.

Finally another agreement of sorts was reached. The leaders of New Brunswick and Manitoba promised to present the pact to their legislatures for all-but-certain ratification. Newfoundland also acquiesced in this plan, but with the reservation that its approval be conferred only after a "free vote" (i.e., one not directed by party discipline) among legislators in the provincial House of Assembly.

One week before the deadline for passage of Meech Lake, legal technicalities and the manoeuvres of Elijah Harper, a maverick New Democrat and Cree Native, stalled the accord in the Manitoba Legislative Assembly. He insisted that the agreement overlooked the needs of Aboriginal peoples in Canada. As it turned out, neither the Manitoba nor the Newfoundland legislatures brought the measure to a vote before the deadline, thereby driving a stake through the heart of the three-year-old Meech Lake accord.

"MAIL YOUR LETTERS RIGHT AWAY!"

Stung by this defeat, Mulroney's strategists adopted a funereal tone and withdrew temporarily from fashioning constitutional deals. The leader of the opposition was less alarmed by the negative consequences predicted with the death of the accord. Liberal Jean Chrétien warned Canadians to resist a midsummer funk and recommended that they resume the important seasonal business of following baseball scores.

In Quebec, convinced separatists and diehard federalists heaved, in unison, a heavy sigh of relief. But those who occupied the middle ground on questions of nationalism were left alone —dangerously—to sulk. A florid, if ahistorical, resentment over the demise of the agreement simmered in Quebec. This reaction was piled atop the fable of the province's "humiliation" in the negotiations that led to repatriation of the Constitution in 1982.

But the gambler who confessed to guiding the premiers to the constitutional brink with a "roll of the dice" could not stay away from the intergovernmental gaming tables for long. Like an addict, Mulroney craved another dose of the highly refined stuff of statesmanship that had given him his most potent political high — and the nation a protracted emotional crash.

"In the constitutional negotiations which have been ongoing since 1987," Trudeau and his former assistant, Thomas Axworthy, assert in the revised edition of the book that they edited, *Towards a Just Society*, "the federal government's position has been all tactics and no vision. Get a deal, any deal, pretty well sums up the story." They credit Mulroney with having "mediated between the provinces," but they blame him for taking up this sensitive task with "no fixed views of his own." To the contrary, "since 1984," they argue, "Mulroney has been willing to discuss dealing away virtually any federal power in exchange for a constitutional settlement. No premier has asked for the Post Office yet," they add sarcastically, "but if they do, mail your letters right away!"

The daring of Mulroney's constitutional compulsion was rivalled only by its redundancy. To pursue his compulsion was to impose highly charged solutions of the present moment on traditional problems. Trudeau and Axworthy note as much: "Canada is a success, looking for a problem," they observe. "We are a united people divided by our leaders."

THE CHARLOTTETOWN AGREEMENT

Two years after the Meech Lake accord perished, the Mulroney government presented Canadians with another blueprint for constitutional reform. This try at renewal was popularly known as the Charlottetown agreement, after the capital city of Prince Edward Island, where the deal was assembled. It was at Charlottetown that the Fathers of Confederation converged in September 1864 to begin uniting disparate pieces of North America under British supervision into the country that became Canada. In August 1992, more than 125 years later, provincial and territorial leaders and representatives of Canada's Native inhabitants (or "First Peoples") convened in Charlottetown to revise and restate the terms that knit them together as a nation.

In some respects, the constitutional package that they devised was original; in others, it borrowed substantially from proposals initiated at Meech Lake. In nearly every respect, it was controversial. Mary Janigan's careful dissection of the deal in *Maclean's* noted that "it offers no inspiring national vision." Like the nineteenth-century Fathers of Confederation, the modern representatives who met in Charlottetown, she wrote, "embraced often-contradictory understandings of the nation."

Among the new features was a so-called "Canada Clause," a list of "fundamental characteristics" of Canada as a nation and Canadians as its citizens. But under the cover of this novel concept, the line from the Meech Lake accord that recognized Quebec as a "distinct society" was recycled and would have been introduced permanently into the Constitution. Moreover, the new context would have obligated governments not merely to legislate equality between speakers of the two official languages, but also to promote minority communities defined by linguistic homogeneity. The Charlottetown agreement thus promised to move Canada further from a commitment to protecting an individual's basic rights and closer to defending — even developing — a group's interests.

This emphasis on the priority of the collectivity could easily be detected in another set of provisions in the Charlottetown agreement: a plan for the reallocation of representation in Parliament along the lines of group membership. It was, to say the least, a potential remedy relatively new to recent Canadian constitutional discourse. Parliament's upper house, the Senate, would have been transformed into an elected body, with six seats for each province, one for each territory, and an undetermined number for Aboriginals, a group not demarcated by geographical boundaries. Provinces would have been permitted to bypass the electorate and select their senators indirectly through a vote in their legislatures. They could have required, furthermore, that Senate delegations include equal numbers of men and women. In the reorganized Senate, approval for bills relating to French language or culture would have required a dual majority. That is, passage would have taken a majority of all members and majority of votes cast by French-speaking senators.

On the lower level, in the House of Commons, the Charlottetown agreement dictated that at least one quarter of the seats be reserved in perpetuity for members from Quebec, an officially francophone province, regardless of Canada's demographic profile in the future. Additionally the agreement revived another Meech-round holdover: Quebec's right to compose a pool of nominees from which three of the nine justices of the Supreme Court of Canada would be appointed. It would also have extended some political autonomy to Aboriginal peoples, including a right of linguistic and cultural preservation and promotion similar to the assurances that Quebec had won.

FIGHTING THE LAST WAR?

Although the leaders had endorsed its terms, the Charlottetown agreement was subjected to a national, nonbinding referendum on 26 October 1992, almost two months after the first ministers had reached consensus on its provisions. As with the Meech Lake accord, Pierre Trudeau sprang into action by firing an opening salvo under his byline. This time his medium was the weekly news magazine.

In late September, he was a month away from the publication of the expanded paperback edition of his and Axworthy's best-selling book, *Towards a Just Society*. Yet he released a chapter that he had intended to append to this volume of essays, a general critique of Quebec's constitutional manoeuvring, as "Trudeau Speaks Out." It appeared as a feature essay in the English-language periodical *Maclean's*, and he placed a French version simultaneously in *L'actualité*.

Trudeau's attack did not explicitly target the Charlottetown agreement, but just as the agreement incorporated significant elements of the Meech Lake accord, Trudeau's essay repeated prominent themes from earlier debate over the failed initiative. Quebec nationalists were insular and immature; Quebec's "humiliation" and "betrayal" in previous negotiations were contrived and theatrical; its government was an agent of political "blackmail"; the other provinces were selfishly grabbing for federal powers; the existing Constitution was sufficient for present conditions and future challenges; Prime Minister Mulroney and the federal contingent were pusillanimous and hopelessly impotent; hence, Canada as a nation was imperilled.

Trudeau's denunciation of Quebec's political poses, Tom Fennell and Barry Came pointed out, immediately "vaulted" his opinions "to the forefront of the constitutional debate." Although *Maclean's* supplemented its usual press run, the issue sold out on newsstands only hours after its delivery. Photocopies of the article circulated in some cities for one dollar apiece, *Maclean's* reported. Interest in the source of Trudeau's outburst was felt elsewhere, too. On currency markets, the Canadian dollar dropped more than one cent against its American counterpart.

However, the response from élites to Trudeau's accusations was, if anything, more vitriolic the second time around. Particularly common, as Fennell and Came observed, was the condemnation of Trudeau as "yesterday's man, whose ideas are outmoded." The influential *Globe and Mail* of Toronto entitled a front-page analysis of the essay's impact "Trudeau Sings Old Tune": the former prime minister, Hugh Winsor suggested, "may turn out to be a general fighting the last war." Coverage in the French-language press was more serious, though no more respectful. *Le devoir* of Montreal did not describe Trudeau's position so much as relay dismissals of it. Chantal Hébert's article headlined Quebec Premier Robert Bourassa's rebuttal that Trudeau's thinking on federalism had "not evolved" since the 1970s. The story's inside "jump" carried a retort to Trudeau from Saskatchewan's premier, Roy Romanow, who, as the attorney-general of the province, was his constitutional ally. "This time," the article quoted Romanow as saying, "he is missing the boat."

The first chapter in the second edition of *Towards a Just Society*, written shortly after the constitutional agreement at Charlottetown, surfaced next. Here Trudeau and Axworthy treated the pact in passing. They commented that "the First Ministers have come to an agreement that enshrines much of the Meech Lake Accord plus," among other innovations, "an equal, partially elected and not very effective Senate." Their fairly mild mention ended with a call for a national referendum on the constitutional deal. "On constitution making we place our faith in the people. People, not governments, are sovereign, so it is the people who should decide."

INDIVIDUAL RIGHTS AND COLLECTIVE WRONGS

The truly mortal thrust into the heart of the Charlottetown agreement had not yet occurred. Pierre Trudeau saved most of his verbal ammunition for a deconstruction of the accord before a lively audience at a Chinese restaurant in Montreal on 1 October, three weeks before the national vote. The occasion was a benefit for a rejuvenated *Cité libre*. Speaking without an advance text but holding a copy of the *Consensus Report on the Constitution* as a prop, Trudeau told listeners to a provincewide radio broadcast and four hundred diners — both supportive and critical — that the constitutional "consensus" was a "mess" that "deserves a big NO."

In the printed transcription of his speech, issued under that title, he asserts, "It is no small matter to know whether we are going to live in a society in which personal rights, individual rights, take precedence over collective rights. It is no minor question of secondary importance to know whether we are going to live in a society in which all citizens are equal before the law and before the State itself." The reason is that "When each citizen is not equal to all other citizens in the state, we are faced with a dictatorship, which arranges citizens in a hierarchy according to their beliefs."

According to the columnist Lysiane Gagnon, Trudeau spoke with "a merciless precision and a clarity of mind that no current politician could even hope to emulate." But the political establishment struck back. Richard Mackie quotes Bob Rae, the premier of Ontario, as branding Trudeau "an 'extremely petty' politician" who, in his Montreal speech, had spun a web of "cheap shots, cheap polemics, [and] cheap rhetoric combined with arguments" that were "intellectually dishonest." From Ontario's capital, the *Globe and Mail* sternly agreed with Rae. Trudeau's distaste for the concept of "collective rights," an editorial, entitled "Angry Untruths from a 'Man of Reason,' " maintained, had no bearing on the Charlottetown agreement. The editorial accused him of purveying "untruths" about the accord and formulating "ill-founded" objections. Anger motivated his speech, the editors charged: "His anger obscures the truth and hurts the nation."

Apparently Canadians did not share the *Globe*'s fears. In the popular balloting of 26 October, the Charlottetown agreement was defeated in six of the ten provinces. Quebec, where both separatists and federalists opposed the package, voted no.

SEPARATISM IN DEED

The Meech Lake accord and the Charlottetown agreement justifiably worried Trudeau. If either package had been enacted, it would have given new and untried authority to provincial governments, thereby strengthening the already powerful centrifugal forces within Confederation. In exchange for this sacrifice, Ottawa would have received Quebec's signature on the Constitution. But this signature would have enshrined Quebec in a special position, one that francophone nationalists have sought, and federal governments have denied, for decades.

The Meech Lake and Charlottetown texts acknowledged, not entirely innocently, a patent fact: that Quebec is "a distinct society." In doing so, however, they encouraged its estrangement from the rest of Canada. This recognition would have paved the way ultimately for sovereignty by gradually reducing Quebec's reliance on the central government. The administrative autonomy that each pact granted to Quebec would have rehearsed it for eventual independence. Finally, and most tragically, passage of either agreement would have prepared the rest of Canada for silent absorption into the wider American sphere. For separatism, in deed if not in word, would do more than tear Quebec from Canada: it would leave Canada to tear itself apart piece by piece.

In "Destroying Canada in Order to Save It," Peter Newman quotes Gil Rémillard, the Quebec minister for intergovernmental affairs, as confessing that he "never understood" Trudeau's opposition to the Meech Lake accord. Rémillard "saw Meech Lake as a natural extension of Trudeau's 1982 Constitution — just finishing the unfinished." Yet the Meech Lake agreement, without greater elaboration and judicial testing, appeared to roll back much of what Trudeau thought he had achieved with the reformed Canadian Constitution in 1982. To its credit, Ottawa in the Mulroney years had finally gained from Quebec a pledge to enter fully into the constitutional covenant. But this commitment was offered largely on the latter's terms. To win this

FIGURE 17

*International honours: at the May 1982 commencement of the
University of Notre Dame, Trudeau is awarded an honorary Doctor
of Laws degree. At right is the Rev. Theodore Hesburgh, CSC, American
Catholic leader and then president of Notre Dame. Cambridge University
physicist Stephen Hawking, also honoured, appears in the centre.*

FIGURE 18

Movies and martial arts: sporting a casual shirt and a full beard,
Trudeau attends the August 1993 première in Montreal of a documentary
film series based on his memoirs. Afterwards, he repels an insistent
questioner (actor Pierre Brassard of the satirical Quebec television
program Taquinons la planète*) with a slap to the face. When that*
gesture fails, Trudeau resorts to what the press terms a "well-placed"
karate-style kick to Brassard's "genital parts." Members of
Trudeau's staff insist that the kick did no harm.

concession, furthermore, Mulroney's government had to promise the provinces powers that, ironically, weakened the national union that the Constitution was designed to strengthen.

"He's making Canada what the premiers want it to be," Robert Fulford charged of Mulroney. And what is their version of a nation? It is "a collection of ten independent duchies with a central clearing house in Ottawa for tax collection, foreign relations, and our fitful gestures in the direction of defence." Earlier Fulford said:

> Because Mulroney has few views of his own, and doesn't hold them with much conviction, he's able to reflect our national politics in pure form. Compromise has been the specialty of Canadian prime ministers for 120 years — without it they couldn't have kept the country in one piece — but none of them has compromised with the breathtaking audacity of Mulroney.

The Meech Lake accord and the Charlottetown agreement are thus painfully if typically Canadian: a consensus, an appearance of unity, was reached at the cost of gutting the specific obligations that the pacts would otherwise imply. Their provisions retained little of the high meaning that might have motivated compliance, and none of the raw power that might have coerced it. The unhappy result in both cases was that a symbol of common purpose for Canadians became a demonstration of the improbability of their holding anything in common. Twice again, a discussion of the ultimate aim of Canadian nationhood was averted.

''A GENERATION TOO SOON''?

Pierre Trudeau's political philosophy is to a Canadian national vision what a materialist cast of mind — harsh, severe, and debunking — is to spirituality: parched and infertile ground. In diminishing the symbolic aspect of statecraft (and other less concrete aspects of government), Trudeau reduced problems of leadership to tasks for administration and rationalized the desire for national community into an insistence on undirected personal liberty.

Why this has come from a man who is arguably the most reflective and subtle political thinker in Canada in recent history is not clear. Some responsibility lies in aspects of Trudeau's biography: his privileged upbringing and world travels; his contempt, acquired early in life, for superstition; his instruction in the beauty of the intellect; and his sympathy for social engagement welded, curiously, to a deep and immutable loneliness. Certainly these influences have had their impact.

However, we must recognize the social context in which Trudeau has lived. His personal experiences aside, his potential for achievement as a Canadian leader was circumscribed from the start by a political culture that reinforced his predisposition to rough out pragmatic solutions to perennial problems without appealing to the highest spirit of Canadians. No one in Canadian political life has examined the soul of his people with greater seriousness than Trudeau; but no one has so shunned public mention of its existence.

"Perhaps Pierre Trudeau came a generation too soon," television interviewer Robert MacNeil wistfully suggests, ruminating about the constitutional confusion in Canada today. "No other Canadian has created the political excitement he did for a while, but his flame was for another day." Yet if we believe the results of opinion research, that flame has not been extinguished; it smoulders within the collective memory. In a national poll conducted during March 1992 by Environics, George Bain notes in "The Perils of Poll-Driven Journalism," Trudeau topped a list of a dozen Canadian leaders whom the public was asked to evaluate as constitutional problem-solvers. The incumbent prime minister, Brian Mulroney, placed last.

In "Canadian and American Friendship," an address before a rare joint session of the United States Congress in 1977, Prime

Minister Trudeau repeated, in strikingly basic terms, his opposition to the trappings of nationalism. He quoted the American revolutionary Tom Paine, who declares, in *Rights of Man* (1792), "My country is the world, and my religion is to do good." A worthy sentiment, but one better suited to a patriot such as Paine, who had already won for himself a nation. In the meantime, Canadians manifest what MacNeil describes as "a pathetic hunger for a national spirit, but there is no political will or talent apparent to satisfy it."

"English Canadians [i.e., federalists] should build a country and then maybe we would want to be part of it," Richard Gwyn quotes the Quebec separatist Pierre Bourgault as saying. "Be creative, believe in yourselves, and maybe then we'll believe in you too."

CHRONOLOGY

1919   Joseph Philippe Pierre Yves Elliott Trudeau is born on 18 October in Montreal, the second child and first son (to survive childbirth) of Jean-Charles Emile Trudeau and Grace Elliott Trudeau.

1935   Charles-Emile Trudeau dies on 10 April in a hospital in Orlando, five days after contracting pneumonia. He was forty-seven.

1940   Trudeau receives a baccalaureate degree with honours from the Collège Jean-de-Brébeuf in Montreal.

1940–43   He studies law at the Université de Montréal. In his spare time, he achieves recognition as a skier.

1943   Graduating with honours, Trudeau is called to the bar of Quebec.

1944–45   Having left Canada for the United States, he earns an MA in political economy from Harvard University.

1946–48   Trudeau studies at the École libre des sciences politiques in Paris and the London School of Economics.

1948–49   With a knapsack and walking stick, Trudeau travels through Europe, the Middle East, and southern Asia.

1949   Returning to Canada, Trudeau allies himself with asbestos workers in the Eastern Townships of Quebec who have been on strike since 13 February. He is arrested by provincial police on 22 April and detained for a short time.

1949–51   Trudeau is a junior economist in the Privy Council office in Ottawa from 7 September 1949 to 28 October 1951.

1950   In June, he collaborates to establish and edit the political review Cité libre.

1951–55   Trudeau visits western Europe, the Soviet Union, Africa, and Asia.

1956   From 9 August to 5 September, Professor Frank R. Scott of McGill University and Trudeau paddle down the Mackenzie River in the Northwest Territories. Le Rassemblement démocratique, a coalition of beleaguered left-wing groups in Quebec, is founded on 8 September with Trudeau's help. He serves as vice president. Published in October is *La grève de l'amiante* (*The Asbestos Strike*), Trudeau's extensive study of conditions surrounding the miners' strike at Asbestos.

1958   His pointed analysis of French-Canadian political culture, "Some Obstacles to Democracy in Quebec," is published in August in the *Canadian Journal of Economics and Political Science*.

1960   On 30 April, Trudeau and two friends attempt to canoe from Florida to Cuba. High winds force them to abort the crossing after they cover eighty kilometres. The reformist Quebec Liberal Party under Jean Lesage wins power on 22 June and begins *"la Révolution tranquille"* ("the Quiet Revolution"). With a delegation of Canadian intellectuals and labour activists (including his friend, the Montreal publisher Jacques Hébert), Trudeau tours the People's Republic of China from 13 September to 22 October.

1961   Hébert and Trudeau produce *Deux innocents en Chine rouge* (*Two Innocents in Red China*), a wry and witty account of their journey. Trudeau becomes an associate professor at the Université de Montréal in September. He specializes in civil liberties and constitutional law, and affiliates with the Institut de recherches en droit public.

1964   "Manifeste pour une politique fonctionelle" ("An Appeal for Realism in Politics") appears in May.

1965   Trudeau's "Federalism, Nationalism, and Reason" is published as one contribution to a volume of views on

The Future of Canadian Federalism. Jean Marchand, Gérard Pelletier, and Trudeau convene a press conference on 10 September to announce their candidacies as Liberals for seats in the House of Commons. On 8 November, Trudeau comfortably wins election to the Commons from the Quebec riding of Mount Royal.

1966   In January, Prime Minister Lester Bowles Pearson chooses Trudeau as his parliamentary secretary.

1967   On 4 April, Pearson places Trudeau in his cabinet as minister of justice and attorney-general of Canada. Trudeau undertakes major revisions of law in family and domestic relations, and defends federal government positions in discussions about reform of the Canadian constitution. He introduces an omnibus bill of amendments to the Criminal Code on 20 December. He meets his future wife, Margaret Joan Sinclair of North Vancouver, for the first time during a waterskiing holiday at Christmas on the island of Mooréa in Tahiti. He had sought this refuge in order to contemplate running for the leadership of the Liberal Party. "Trudeaumania" (as the headline writers dub popular fascination with the would-be candidate) gathers momentum in Canada.

1968   On 16 February, Trudeau declares his candidacy for the leadership of the Liberal Party of Canada. *Federalism and the French Canadians*, the English edition of Trudeau's writings on nationalism and related political subjects, is published in March. On 6 April, the Liberal Party, at a convention in Ottawa, names Trudeau its leader on the fourth ballot. Pearson tenders his resignation on 20 April, and Trudeau becomes the fifteenth prime minister of Canada. He leads the Liberal Party to overwhelming victory in a federal election on 25 June. The Liberals win 155 of the 264 seats in the House of Commons, including Trudeau's own.

1969   On 9 July, Parliament adopts the Official Languages Act, legislating English-French bilingualism in federal operations.

1970   Members of the Front de libération du Québec (FLQ) kidnap British trade commissioner James "Jasper" Cross in Montreal on 5 October; it is the opening act in a chain of events that would be called "the October Crisis." Pierre Laporte, the Quebec minister of labour and immigration and deputy premier of the province, is kidnapped on 10 October. The Quebec government requests the imposition of the War Measures Act five days later. After consideration by the federal cabinet, the act is promulgated the following day. Trudeau is criticized for suspending protection of civil liberties. Authorities find Laporte in the trunk of a parked car on 17 October, dead from strangulation. The FLQ claims to have "executed" him. Another set of political essays by Trudeau, *Les cheminements de la politique* (*Approaches to Politics*), is published in November. On 3 December, Cross is freed after fifty-nine days of captivity; his FLQ kidnappers flee to Cuba. Suspects in the murder of Laporte are arrested on 28 December.

1971   In a private Roman Catholic ceremony on 4 March, Trudeau marries Margaret Sinclair, the fourth of five daughters of James Sinclair, a former minister of fisheries in the Liberal government of Prime Minister Louis St. Laurent. The groom is fifty-one, and the bride is twenty-two; it is the first marriage for each partner. Margaret Trudeau thus becomes the youngest first lady in the world. The couple honeymoons briefly in British Columbia. Their first child, Justin Pierre James, is born on Christmas day.

1972   Although Trudeau's popularity is sagging, the Liberal Party retains power in a closely fought federal election on 30 October. Yet the Liberals win a majority of seats only in Quebec. As a minority in the Commons, they govern in concert with the leftist New Democratic Party (NDP).

1973 Trudeau's mother dies on 16 January at eighty-two. Another son, Alexandre Emmanuel ("Sacha"), is also born on Christmas day.

1974 On 8 May, the NDP, with support from the opposition Progressive Conservatives, wins a vote of no-confidence against the Liberal government. Voters restore the Liberals to a parliamentary majority on 8 July; they control more than 140 seats in the new House. Margaret Trudeau enters Royal Victoria Hospital in Montreal on 9 September for treatment of psychiatric ailments. She remains an inpatient for about two weeks.

1975 Michel Charles-Emile ("Micha") is born on 2 October.

1976 On 15 November, Quebec voters elect a separatist government, the Parti québécois, under former broadcast journalist René Lévesque.

1977 On 27 May, the Trudeaus announce their agreement to live "separate and apart." Pierre retains custody of their three children.

1979 *Beyond Reason*, a book ghost written for Margaret Trudeau by British author Caroline Moorehead, is published in April in Canada. Part autobiography and part exposé of her marriage, it describes Pierre as authoritarian, cold, and stingy. On 22 May, the Conservatives defeat the Liberals in a federal election, and Trudeau resigns as prime minister on 4 June. Succeeded by Joe Clark, he becomes leader of the opposition in Parliament. On 21 November, he reveals his intention to resign as leader of the Liberal Party and retire from public life. Pierre's marriage to Margaret experiences its "final break." On 13 December, the government of Joe Clark falls after defeat on a budgetary vote in the House of Commons. Within a week, Trudeau decides to stay on and lead the Liberals in the next election campaign.

1980   The Liberals win the election on 18 February, and on 3 March Trudeau is sworn in again as prime minister. With less than a week to go in the Quebec referendum campaign, he speaks at a rally of "No" forces in Montreal on 14 May. In the provincial referendum on 20 May, nearly three in five Quebeckers say "No" to "sovereignty-association" with Canada.

1981   The Parti québécois is reelected as the government of Quebec on 13 April. The Supreme Court of Canada decides on 28 September that a unanimous endorsement from the provinces is not necessary before a new constitutional package is referred back to the British Parliament. First ministers from nine of the ten provinces agree on 5 November on a mechanism for repatriating the Canadian constitution from Great Britain. Premier René Lévesque of Quebec cries foul.

1982   With Queen Elizabeth II participating, the constitution is returned to Canada in a rain-soaked ceremony on Parliament Hill in Ottawa on 17 April.

1984   On 29 February, Trudeau announces his decision to retire from politics. Upon obtaining a divorce from Pierre, Margaret Trudeau weds Fried Kemper, an Ottawa real-estate developer, in a civil ceremony on 18 April. Trudeau officially resigns as leader of the Liberal Party of Canada on 16 June. John Napier Turner, the new Liberal leader, succeeds him as prime minister on 30 June.

1985   Trudeau is named a Companion of the Order of Canada in November.

1987   On 30 April, in a closed-door meeting at a federal government conference centre near Meech Lake in Quebec, Canada's eleven first ministers reach agreement on a series of amendments to the constitution, one of which recognizes Quebec as "a distinct society." On 27 May, in Montreal and Toronto newspapers, Trudeau publishes an open letter that is highly derisive of

Prime Minister Brian Mulroney and the premiers who negotiated the constitutional accord at Meech Lake. The final form of the accord is drafted during a meeting on 3 June at the Langevin Block in Ottawa. To be enacted, the accord must be approved within three years by Parliament and the legislatures of all ten provinces. On 27 August, Trudeau criticizes the accord before a joint committee of the House of Commons and the Senate.

1988   Trudeau again speaks out against the Meech Lake accord, this time before the Senate on 30 March.

1990   *Towards a Just Society*, a chronicle of the policy achievements of "the Trudeau years," edited by Trudeau and his former principal secretary, Thomas Axworthy, is published on 20 March. The closing chapter, by Trudeau, contains a trenchant critique of the Mulroney government in shaping the Meech Lake accord. Stalled in the Manitoba legislature by the protests of Aboriginal leaders, and not brought to a vote in the Newfoundland House of Assembly, the Meech Lake accord expires on 23 June without being ratified.

1991   Sarah Elisabeth is born on 5 May to Deborah Coyne, a law professor and advisor on constitutional affairs to the government of Newfoundland and Labrador; newspapers report that the child's birth certificate identifies Trudeau as the father. On 24 September, the Conservative government tables proposals for the constitutional renewal of Canadian federalism.

1992   On 28 August, after a series of meetings in Charlottetown, Prince Edward Island, Mulroney, the ten provincial premiers, the two territorial leaders, and representatives of Canada's first peoples approve the text of an agreement to attempt once again an overhaul of the constitution. In a cover essay for the 28 September issues of *Maclean's* and *L'actualité*, Trudeau assails proposals for new constitutional arrangements as abandoning the principles of Canadian federalism. The following day, newspaper analysts dismiss his criticisms; one compares him to "a general fighting the last war"; Quebec Premier Robert Bourassa asserts that Trudeau's thinking on federalism has exhibited "no evolution" over more than two decades. Speaking on 1 October at La Maison Egg Roll, a Chinese restaurant in Montreal, Trudeau tells patrons of *Cité libre* that the Charlottetown agreement is "a mess that deserves a big NO." In a nonbinding popular vote on 26 October, the Charlottetown agreement suffers clear defeat in six provinces (including Quebec) and one territory.

1993   Attending the Montreal Festival des films du monde (World Film Festival), Trudeau is in the audience for the première on 30 August of the first segment of a five-part documentary based on his forthcoming memoirs. After the screening, he is involved in a brief altercation with Pierre Brassard, a Quebec television actor who impersonates a newsman. On 9 November, Trudeau embarks on a two-week author tour to promote the long-awaited publication of his memoirs. The trip takes him from Montreal to Ottawa, Toronto, Edmonton, and Vancouver.

WORKS CONSULTED

Acton, John Emerich Edward Dahlberg. "Nationality." *Essays on Freedom and Power*. By Acton. Ed. Gertrude Himmelfarb. New York: Meridian, 1955. 141–70.

"Amendments Framed 'to Foster Greater Harmony.'" *Globe and Mail* [Toronto] 4 June 1987: A10.

"Angry Untruths from a 'Man of Reason.'" Editorial. *Globe and Mail* [Toronto] 3 Oct. 1992: D6.

Axworthy, Thomas S., and Pierre Elliott Trudeau. "The Tempest Bursting: Canada in 1992." Axworthy and Trudeau, rev. ed. 7–50.

———, eds. *Towards a Just Society: The Trudeau Years*. Trans. Patricia Claxton. Markham, ON: Viking-Penguin, 1990.

———, eds. *Towards a Just Society: The Trudeau Years*. Rev. ed. Trans. Patricia Claxton. Toronto: Penguin, 1992.

Bain, George. "Canada Has a Case of Trudeaumania." *New York Times Magazine* 16 June 1968: 10+.

———. "The Perils of Poll-Driven Journalism." *Maclean's* 20 Apr. 1992: 44.

Balthazar, Louis. "Quebec at the Hour of Choice." Carty and Ward 60–75.

Balthazar, Louis, Guy Laforest, and Vincent Lemieux, eds. *Le Québec et la restructuration du Canada, 1980–1992: Enjeux et perspectives*. Sillery, PQ: Septentrion, 1991.

Behiels, Michael D., ed. *The Meech Lake Primer: Conflicting Views of the 1987 Constitutional Accord*. Ottawa: U of Ottawa P, 1989.

———. *Prélude to Quebec's Quiet Revolution: Liberalism versus Neo-Nationalism, 1945–1960*. Montreal: McGill-Queen's UP, 1985.

Bélanger, André-J. *Ruptures et constantes: Quatre idéologies du Québec en éclatement: La relève, La JEC, Cité libre, Parti pris*. Montréal: Éditions HMH, 1977.

Bélanger, Yves, et al. *L'ère des libéraux: Le pouvoir fédéral de 1963 à 1984*. Sillery, PQ: P de l'U du Québec, 1988.

Bellah, Robert N. "Civil Religion in America." *Daedalus* 96 (1967): 1–21.

Bergeron, Gérard. "Foreign Affairs." *The Canadians: 1867–1967*. Ed. J.M.S. Careless and R. Craig Brown. New York: St. Martin's, 1967. 785–805.

———. *Incertitudes d'un certain pays: Le Québec et le Canada dans le monde (1958–1978)*. Québec: P de l'U Laval, 1979.

———. *Notre miroir à deux faces: Trudeau, Lévesque*. Montréal: Québec-Amérique, 1985.

———. "Les partis politiques québécois à la fin de la période duplessiste." Bergeron, *Incertitudes* 91–110.

———. "Political Parties in Quebec." *University of Toronto Quarterly* 27 (1958): 352–68.

———. "Un siècle d'histoire (1867–1967), mais moins d'un quart de siècle de politique étrangère (1945–1967)." Bergeron, *Incertitudes* 13–30.

Beyer, Peter. "Roman Catholicism in Contemporary Quebec: The Ghosts of Religion Past?" *The Sociology of Religion: A Canadian Focus*. Ed. W.E. Hewitt. Toronto: Butterworths, 1993. 133–56.

Bibby, Reginald W. *Mosaic Madness: The Poverty and Potential of Life in Canada*. Toronto: Stoddart, 1990.

Black, Conrad. *Duplessis*. Toronto: McClelland, 1977.

Bliss, Michael. "Privatizing the Mind: The Sundering of Canadian History, the Sundering of Canada." *Journal of Canadian Studies/Revue d'études canadiennes* 26.4 (1991–92): 5–17.

Bom, Philip C. *Trudeau's Canada: Truth and Consequences*. St. Catharines: Guardian, 1977.

Bordeleau, Charles, comp. *Pierre Elliott Trudeau*. Saint-Lambert, PQ: Éditions héritage, 1978.

Botting, Gary. *Fundamental Freedoms and Jehovah's Witnesses*. Calgary: U of Calgary P, 1993.

Bowker, Marjorie Montgomery. *Canada's Constitutional Crisis: Making Sense of It All (A Background Analysis and Look at the Future)*. Edmonton: Lone Pine, 1991.

———. *The Meech Lake Accord: What It Will Mean to You and to Canada: An Independent Analysis*. Hull, PQ: Voyageur, 1990.

Breton, Albert, et al. "An Appeal for Realism in Politics." *Canadian Forum* May 1964: 29–33.

Brittain, Donald. "The Champions." *Boundaries of Identity: A Quebec Reader.* Ed. William Dodge. Toronto: Lester, 1992. 45–62.

Broadbent, Ed. *The Liberal Rip-Off: Trudeauism vs. the Politics of Equality.* Toronto: New, 1970.

Brunelle, Dorval. *Les trois colombes: Essai.* Montréal: VLB éditeur, 1985.

Burgess, Michael. "Meech Lake: The Process of Constitutional Reform in Canada, 1987–90." *British Journal of Canadian Studies* 5 (1990): 275–96.

Burns, John F. "Canada Accord on Quebec Issue May Fall Apart: Agreement Announced, Then Mired in Dispute." *New York Times* 10 June 1990: 1, 9.

———. "Canadian Leaders Sign Quebec Pact: Doubts Remain on Whether 3 Provinces Will Approve It." *New York Times* 11 June 1990: A1, A7.

———. "Trudeau Returns, and the Reception Is Mixed." *New York Times* 29 Aug. 1987: 1, 4.

———. "With Canada's Future in Question, Newfoundland Ponders a Vital Vote." *New York Times* 18 June 1990: A3.

Cahill, Jack. *John Turner: The Long Run.* Toronto: McClelland, 1984.

Canada. *Consensus Report on the Constitution: Charlottetown, August 28, 1992, Final Text.* Rpt. as "The Consensus Report on the Constitution." *Globe and Mail* [Toronto] 3 Oct. 1992: A8–10.

———. Parliament. Special Joint Committee of the Senate and of the House of Commons. *Minutes of Proceedings and Evidence of the Special Joint Committee of the Senate and of the House of Commons on the 1987 Constitutional Accord: Issue No. 14 (Thursday, August 27, 1987).* Ottawa: Queen's Printer, 1987.

———. *Report: The 1987 Constitutional Accord.* Ottawa: Queen's Printer, 1987.

———. Royal Commission on Bilingualism and Biculturalism. *A Preliminary Report of the Royal Commission on Bilingualism and Biculturalism.* Ottawa: Queen's Printer, 1965.

Carstairs, Sharon. "Why the Meech Lake Accord Must Be Torpedoed." *Canadian Speeches* Feb. 1989: 17–21.

Carty, R. Kenneth, and W. Peter Ward, eds. *Entering the Eighties: Canada in Crisis.* Toronto: Oxford UP, 1980.

Casgrain, Thérèse F. *A Woman in a Man's World.* Trans. Joyce Marshall. Toronto: McClelland, 1972.

Chamberlin, William Henry. *Canada: Today and Tomorrow*. Boston: Little, 1942.

Charney, Ann. "Pierre Elliott Trudeau: The Myth and the Reality." Newman and Fillmore 110–22.

Chrétien, Jean. "Bringing the Constitution Home." Axworthy and Trudeau 282–309.

———. *Straight from the Heart*. Toronto: Key, 1985.

Christiano, Kevin J. "Federalism as a Canadian National Ideal: The Civic Rationalism of Pierre Elliott Trudeau." *Dalhousie Review* 69 (1989): 248–69.

Clark, Gerald. "Trudeau without Trudeaumania: Canada's P.M. Is Not a Simple Swinger Nor a Radical Reformer." *New York Times Magazine* 25 Jan. 1970: 26+.

Clarkson, Stephen, and Christina McCall. *The Magnificent Obsession*. Toronto: McClelland, 1990. Vol. 1 of *Trudeau and Our Times*. 2 vols. 1990–94.

Cochrane, Felicity. *Margaret Trudeau: The Prime Minister's Runaway Wife*. Scarborough: Signet-NAL, 1978.

Cohen, Andrew. *A Deal Undone: The Making and Breaking of the Meech Lake Accord*. Vancouver: Douglas, 1990.

———. "Politics: Trudeau's Child." *Saturday Night* Mar. 1993: 15+.

Cohen, Lenard, Patrick Smith, and Paul Warwick. *The Vision and the Game: Making the Canadian Constitution*. Calgary: Detselig, 1987.

Coleman, William D. *The Independence Movement in Quebec, 1945–1980*. Toronto: U of Toronto P, 1984.

Comeau, Pauline. "The Man Who Said No." *Canadian Forum* July-Aug. 1990: 7–11.

Confédération des syndicats nationaux (CSN), and Centrale de l'enseignement du Québec (CEQ). Education Committees. *The History of the Labour Movement in Quebec*. Trans. Arnold Bennett. Montreal: Black Rose, 1987.

Cook, Ramsay. "Alice in Meachland, or The Concept of Quebec as 'A Distinct Society.'" *Queen's Quarterly* 94 (1987): 817–28.

———. "'I Never Thought I Could Be as Proud . . .': The Trudeau-Lévesque Debate." Axworthy and Trudeau 342–56.

———. *The Maple Leaf Forever: Essays in Nationalism and Politics in Canada*. Toronto: Macmillan, 1971.

Cox, Kevin. "Will Hold Free Vote on Meech, Wells Says: Possibility of Ratification Rises as Referendum Rejected." *Globe and Mail* [Toronto] 12 June 1990: A1-2.

Coyne, Deborah. *Roll of the Dice: Working with Clyde Wells during the Meech Lake Negotiations*. Toronto: Lorimer, 1992.

Coyne, Deborah, and Robert Howse. *No Deal!: Why Canadians Should Reject the Mulroney Constitution*. Hull, PQ: Voyageur, 1992.

Dagenais, André. *Dissolution de la confédération canadienne*. Montréal: privately printed, 1981. Vol. 1 of *Libérer/renverser*.

Davey, Keith. *The Rainmaker: A Passion for Politics*. Toronto: Stoddart, 1986.

David, Hélène. "La grève et le bon Dieu: La grève de l'amiante au Québec." *Sociologie et sociétés* 1 (1969): 249-76.

Delacourt, Susan. "Legacy Distorted, Mulroney Says: Defence of Record on National Unity Laced with Parting Shots at Trudeau." *Globe and Mail* [Toronto] 29 May 1993: A1, A4.

———. "Senate Has Chance to Kill Meech Deal, Trudeau Suggests." *Globe and Mail* [Toronto] 31 Mar. 1988: A1-2.

———. "Senator Argues against Proposals to Block Pact." *Globe and Mail* [Toronto] 1 Apr. 1988: A5.

Delacourt, Susan, and Graham Fraser. "Marathon Talks Were All Part of Plan, PM Says: Federal Government's Strategy on Holdout Provinces Mapped Out a Month Ago." *Globe and Mail* [Toronto] 12 June 1990: A1, A7.

Denton, Herbert H. "Canadians Amend Constitution to Include Quebec's 'Distinct Society.' " *Washington Post* 4 June 1987: A32.

———. "Trudeau Returns to Parliament Hill: Canada's Retired Crowd Pleaser Defends His Constitution." *Washington Post* 29 Aug. 1987: A12, A24.

Dewey, John. *A Common Faith*. New Haven, CT: Yale UP, 1934.

Dion, Gérard, and Louis O'Neill. *L'immortalité politique dans la province de Québec*. Montréal: Comité de moralité publique, 1956.

Dion, Léon. *Les intellectuels et le temps de Duplessis*. Sainte-Foy, PQ: P de l'U Laval, 1993. Vol. 2 of *Québec, 1945-2000*. 2 vols. 1987-93.

Djwa, Sandra. *The Politics of the Imagination: A Life of F.R. Scott*. Toronto: McClelland, 1987.

Djwa, Sandra, and R. St. J. Macdonald, eds. *On F.R. Scott: Essays on His Contributions to Law, Literature, and Politics*. Montreal: McGill-Queen's UP, 1983.

Donaldson, Gordon. *Eighteen Men: The Prime Ministers of Canada*. Toronto: Doubleday, 1985.

Durham, John George Lambton, Earl of. *Lord Durham's Report: An Abridgement of Report on the Affairs of British North America by Lord Durham*. Ed. Gerald M. Craig. Toronto: McClelland, 1963.

Durocher, René. "Maurice Duplessis et sa conception de l'autonomie provinciale au début de sa carrière politique." *Revue d'histoire de l'Amérique française* 23 (1969): 13–34.

English, John. *The Worldly Years: 1949–1972*. Toronto: Knopf, 1992. Vol. 2 of *The Life of Lester Pearson*. 2 vols. 1989–92.

Fennell, Tom, with Barry Came. "The Trudeau Storm: The Former Leader Provokes a War of Words." *Maclean's* 5 Oct. 1992: 20, 22.

Forsey, Eugene. *A Life on the Fringe: The Memoirs of Eugene Forsey*. Toronto: Oxford UP, 1990.

———. "Under the Padlock." Granatstein and Stevens 157–61.

Foster, W.A. *Canada First; Or, Our New Nationality: An Address*. Toronto: Adam, 1871.

Fournier, Pierre. *A Meech Lake Post-Mortem: Is Quebec Sovereignty Inevitable?* Trans. Sheila Fischman. Montreal: McGill-Queen's UP, 1991.

Franks, C.E.S. *The Myths and Symbols of the Constitutional Debate in Canada*. Reflections Paper 11. Kingston: Inst. of Intergovernmental Relations, Queen's U, 1993.

Fraser, Graham. "Eloquence, Tears, Euphoria, Rage All Part of the 7-Day Meech War." *Globe and Mail* [Toronto] 11 June 1990: A1, A5.

———. "Meech Lake Strengthens Rights, PM Says: Pact 'Broke Constitutional Straightjacket.'" *Globe and Mail* [Toronto] 15 June 1988: A8.

———. *Playing for Keeps: The Making of the Prime Minister, 1988*. Rev. ed. Toronto: McClelland, 1990.

Fulford, Robert. "Notebook: Surrendering Canada." *Saturday Night* Aug. 1987: 5–7.

Gagnon, Lysiane. "Inside Quebec: Credibility of the Yes Side Took a Drubbing All Week Long." *Globe and Mail* [Toronto] 3 Oct. 1992: D3.

Genest, Jean-Guy. "Aspects de l'administration Duplessis." *Revue d'histoire de l'Amérique française* 25 (1971): 389–92.

Gessell, Paul. "Mulroney's Magic Moment." *Maclean's* 15 June 1987: 17.

Gessell, Paul, and Brian Jones. "A Historic 'Yes' Vote." *Maclean's* 9 Nov. 1987: 12.

Gibbins, Roger. "The Interplay of Political Institutions and Political Communities." Shugarman and Whitaker 423–38.

Goddard, John. "Spectator: Pierre Trudeau Bids His Canada Farewell." *Saturday Night* July 1988: 80.

Gordon, Walter L. *A Political Memoir.* Toronto: McClelland, 1977.

Gossage, Patrick. *Close to the Charisma: My Years between the Press and Pierre Elliott Trudeau.* Toronto: McClelland, 1986.

Graham, Ron. *One-Eyed Kings: Promise and Illusion in Canadian Politics.* Don Mills, ON: Collins, 1986.

Granatstein, J.L., and Robert Bothwell. *Pirouette: Pierre Trudeau and Canadian Foreign Policy.* Toronto: U of Toronto P, 1990.

Granatstein, J.L., and Peter Stevens, eds. *Forum: Canadian Life and Letters, 1920–70. Selections from* The Canadian Forum. Toronto: U of Toronto P, 1972.

Grant, George. "Nationalism and Rationality." *Canadian Forum* Jan. 1971: 336–37. Rpt. in Rotstein, *Power Corrupted* 49–56.

Grant, John Webster. *The Church in the Canadian Era.* Burlington, ON: Welch, 1988.

Griffiths, Linda, with Paul Thompson. *Maggie and Pierre: A Fantasy of Love, Politics and the Media.* Vancouver: Talonbooks, 1980.

Guindon, Hubert. *Quebec Society: Tradition, Modernity, and Nationhood.* Ed. Roberta Hamilton and John L. McMullan. Toronto: U of Toronto P, 1988.

———. "The Social Evolution of Quebec Reconsidered." *Canadian Journal of Economics and Political Science* 26 (1960): 533–51.

Gwyn, Richard. *The Northern Magus: Pierre Trudeau and Canadians.* Ed. Sandra Gwyn. Toronto: McClelland, 1980.

Hall, Douglas. *The Canada Crisis: A Christian Perspective.* Toronto: Anglican Book Centre, 1980.

Harbron, John D. *This Is Trudeau.* Don Mills, ON: Longmans, 1968.

Hébert, Chantal, with Pierre O'Neil and Jean Dion. "Trudeau soulève une tempête au Canada, une brise au Québec: Il n'a pas évolué depuis 20 ans, dit Bourassa." *Le devoir* [Montréal] 22 sept. 1992: A-1, A-4.

Hébert, Jacques, and Pierre Elliott Trudeau. *Two Innocents in Red China.* Trans. I.M. Owen. Toronto: Oxford UP, 1968.

Hiemstra, John L. *Trudeau's Political Philosophy: Its Implications for Liberty and Progress*. Toronto: Inst. for Christian Studies, 1983.

Hogg, Peter W. *Meech Lake Constitutional Accord Annotated*. Toronto: Carswell, 1988.

Horton, Donald J. *André Laurendeau: French-Canadian Nationalist, 1912–1968*. Toronto: Oxford UP, 1992.

Hoy, Claire. *Clyde Wells: A Political Biography*. Toronto: Stoddart, 1992.

Hughes, Everett Cherrington. *French Canada in Transition*. Chicago: U of Chicago P, 1943.

Hutchison, Bruce. "Bruce Hutchison Writes an Open Letter to Pierre Elliott Trudeau." Newman and Fillmore 45–58.

Iglauer, Edith. "Profiles: Prime Minister / *Premier ministre*." *New Yorker* 5 July 1969: 36+.

Ignatieff, Michael. "The Longest Shadow." *Saturday Night* Oct. 1987: 25–32.

Ingle, Lorne, ed. *Meech Lake Reconsidered*. Hull, PQ: Voyageur, 1989.

Jamieson, Don. *A World unto Itself*. Ed. Carmelita McGrath. St. John's: Breakwater, 1991. Vol. 2 of *The Political Memoirs of Don Jamieson*. 2 vols. 1989–91.

Janigan, Mary. "A Voter's Handbook for the Referendum: What the Accord Says — and What It Means." *Maclean's* 19 Oct. 1992: 24–29.

Janigan, Mary, et al. "Canada's New Deal." *Maclean's* 15 June 1987: 8–10.

"J.C.E. Trudeau: Was the Largest Stockholder of Montreal Baseball Team." *New York Times* 12 Apr. 1935: 23.

Johnson, Arthur. *Margaret Trudeau*. Markham, ON: PaperJacks, 1977.

Johnston, Donald J., ed. *Pierre Trudeau Speaks Out on Meech Lake*. Toronto: General, 1990.

———. *Up the Hill*. Montreal: Optimum, 1986.

———, ed. *With a Bang, Not a Whimper: Pierre Trudeau Speaks Out*. Toronto: Stoddart, 1988.

Kaplan, William. *State and Salvation: The Jehovah's Witnesses and Their Fight for Civil Rights*. Toronto: U of Toronto P, 1989.

Keate, Stuart. Introduction. *The True Face of Duplessis*. By Pierre Laporte. Montreal: Harvest House, 1960. 9–13.

Keith, J.E. [F.R. Scott]. "The Fascist Province." Granatstein and Stevens 120–22.

Kent, Tom. *A Public Purpose: An Experience of Liberal Opposition and Canadian Government.* Montreal: McGill-Queen's UP, 1988.

Laforest, Guy. *Trudeau et la fin d'un rêve canadien.* Sillery, PQ: Septentrion, 1992.

Laurendeau, André. "One Hundred Pages by Pierre Elliott Trudeau." *André Laurendeau: Witness for Quebec.* Ed. and trans. Philip Stratford. Toronto: Macmillan, 1973. 161–71.

Laxer, James, and Robert Laxer. *The Liberal Idea of Canada: Pierre Trudeau and the Question of Canada's Survival.* Toronto: Lorimer, 1977.

Leith, Linda. *Introducing Hugh MacLennan's Two Solitudes: A Reader's Guide.* Canadian Fiction Studies 10. Toronto: ECW, 1990.

Lemieux, Vincent, and Raymond Hudon, with Nicole Aubé. *Patronage et politique au Québec: 1944–1972.* Sillery, PQ: Éditions du boréal express, 1975.

Lessard, François-J. *Messages au "frère" Trudeau.* Pointe-Fortune, PQ: Éditions de ma grand-mère, 1979.

Lévesque, René. *Memoirs.* Trans. Philip Stratford. Toronto: McClelland, 1986.

McCall-Newman, Christina. *Grits: An Intimate Portrait of the Liberal Party.* Toronto: Macmillan, 1982.

MacDonald, L. Ian. *From Bourassa to Bourassa: A Pivotal Decade in Canadian History.* Montreal: Harvest House, 1984.

MacIntyre, Alasdair. *After Virtue: A Study in Moral Theory.* Notre Dame, IN: U of Notre Dame P, 1981.

Mackie, Richard. " 'Petty' Politician Draws Rae's Fury: Ex-PM Delivered 'Cheap Rhetoric.' " *Globe and Mail* [Toronto] 3 Oct. 1992: A4.

MacLennan, Hugh. *Two Solitudes.* New York: Duell, 1945.

McLeod, Carol. *Wives of the Canadian Prime Ministers.* Hantsport, NS: Lancelot, 1985.

McLuhan, Marshall. "The Story of the Man in the Mask." Rev. of *Federalism and the French Canadians,* by Pierre Trudeau. *New York Times Book Review* 17 Nov. 1968: 36–38.

MacNeil, Robert. "Looking for My Country." *American Review of Canadian Studies* 21 (1991): 409–21.

McRae, Kenneth D. "Empire, Language, and Nation: The Canadian Case." *Analyses by Region.* Ed. S.N. Eisenstadt and Stein Rokkan. Vol. 2 of *Building States and Nations.* Beverly Hills: Sage, 1973. 144–76. 2 vols.

McRoberts, Kenneth. "Making Canada Bilingual: Illusions and Delusions of Federal Language Policy." Shugarman and Whitaker 141–71.

McRoberts, Kenneth, and Dale Posgate. *Quebec: Social Change and Political Crisis.* Rev. ed. Toronto: McClelland, 1980.

Maheux, Arthur. "French Canadians and Democracy." *University of Toronto Quarterly* 27 (1958): 341–51.

Mathews, Robin. "Canadian Culture and the Liberal Ideology." *Canadian Literature: Surrender or Revolution.* By Mathews. Ed. Gail Dexter. Toronto: Steel Rail, 1978. 191–204.

Matthews, Ralph. *The Creation of Regional Dependency.* Toronto: U of Toronto P, 1983.

Miner, Horace. *St. Denis: A French-Canadian Parish.* Chicago: U of Chicago P, 1939.

Monahan, Patrick. *Meech Lake: The Inside Story.* Toronto: U of Toronto P, 1991.

Monière, Denis. *Le développement des idéologies au Québec: Des origines à nos jours.* Montréal: Québec-Amérique, 1977.

Moon, Robert, comp. *PM/Dialogue.* Hull, PQ: High Hill, 1972.

Newman, Peter C. "Destroying Canada in Order to Save It." *Maclean's* 17 Dec. 1990: 44.

———. *A Nation Divided: Canada and the Coming of Pierre Trudeau.* New York: Knopf, 1969.

Newman, Peter C., and Stan Fillmore, eds. *Their Turn to Curtsy — Your Turn to Bow.* Toronto: Maclean-Hunter, 1972.

Nielsen, Erik. *The House Is Not a Home: An Autobiography.* Toronto: Macmillan, 1989.

Oliver, Michael. "Laurendeau et Trudeau: Leurs opinions sur le Canada." *L'engagement intellectuel: Mélanges en honneur de Léon Dion.* Ed. Raymond Hudon and Réjean Pelletier. Sainte-Foy, PQ: P de l'U Laval, 1991. 339–68.

Peacock, Donald. *Journey to Power: The Story of a Canadian Election.* Toronto: Ryerson, 1968.

Pellerin, Jean. *Le phénomène Trudeau.* Paris: Éditions Seghers, 1972.

Pelletier, Gérard. *L'aventure du pouvoir, 1968–1975.* Montréal: Éditions intl. Alain Stanke, 1992.

———. *The October Crisis.* Trans. Joyce Marshall. Toronto: McClelland, 1971.

──── . *Years of Choice: 1960–1968.* Trans. Alan Brown. Toronto: Methuen, 1987.

──── . *Years of Impatience: 1950–1960.* Trans. Alan Brown. New York: Facts on File, 1984.

Powe, B.W. *The Solitary Outlaw.* Toronto: Lester, 1987.

Québec. Conseil exécutif. *Québec-Canada: A New Deal; The Québec Government Proposal for a New Partnership between Equals: Sovereignty-Association.* Québec: Éditeur officiel, 1979.

Quebec Liberal Party. *Choose Québec AND Canada: A Working Document for the Members of the Québec Liberal Party.* Montreal: Quebec Liberal Party, 1979.

──── . Constitutional Committee. *A New Canadian Federation.* Montreal: Quebec Liberal Party, 1980.

Quinn, Herbert F. *The Union Nationale: Quebec Nationalism from Duplessis to Lévesque.* 2nd ed. Toronto: U of Toronto P, 1979.

Radwanski, George. *Trudeau.* New York: Taplinger, 1978.

Resnick, Philip. *Parliament vs. People: An Essay on Democracy and Canadian Political Culture.* Vancouver: New Star, 1984.

Rioux, Marcel. *Pour prendre publiquement congé de quelques salauds.* Montréal: Éditions de l'hexagone, 1980.

Roberts, Leslie. *The Chief: A Political Biography of Maurice Duplessis.* Toronto: Clarke, 1963.

Robertson, Heather. *More Than a Rose: Prime Ministers, Wives and Other Women.* Toronto: Seal-McClelland-Bantam, 1991.

Romanow, Roy, John Whyte, and Howard Leeson. *Canada . . . Notwithstanding: The Making of the Constitution, 1976–1982.* Toronto: Carswell-Methuen, 1984.

Rose, Michael, Marc Clark, and Bruce Wallace. "What Bourassa Won." *Maclean's* 11 May 1987: 11.

Rotstein, Abraham. "Constitution without Tiers?" *Canadian Forum* Mar. 1968: 266–68.

──── , ed. *Power Corrupted: The October Crisis and the Repression of Quebec.* Toronto: New, 1971.

──── . *The Precarious Homestead: Essays on Economics, Technology and Nationalism.* Toronto: New, 1973.

──── . "The Search for Independence." *Canadian Forum* Oct. 1969: 146–48. Rpt. in Granatstein and Stevens 424–28.

Roy, Jean-Louis. *Le choix d'un pays: Le débat constitutionnel Québec-*

Canada, 1960–1976. Ottawa: Éditions Leméac, 1978.

S [F.R. Scott]. "Embryo Fascism in Quebec." *Foreign Affairs* 16 (1938): 454–66.

Sarra-Bournet, Michel. *L'affaire Roncarelli: Duplessis contre les Témoins de Jéhovah*. Collection Edmond-de-Nevers 5. Québec: Inst. québécois de recherche sur la culture, 1986.

Savoie, Claude. *Les crises de Pierre Elliott Trudeau*. Montréal: Éditions scriptomédia, 1979.

Schlesinger, Arthur M., Jr. *The Vital Center: The Politics of Freedom*. Boston: Houghton, 1949.

Scott, F.R. "Areas of Conflict in the Field of Public Law and Policy." *Canadian Dualism/La dualité canadienne: Studies of French-English Relations*. Ed. Mason Wade. Toronto: U of Toronto P; Québec: P de l'U Laval, 1960. 81–105.

———. *Civil Liberties and Canadian Federalism*. Toronto: U of Toronto P, 1959.

Séguin, Rhéal. "Value of Distinct-Society Clause Not Known, Quebec Acknowledges: Minister Says Province Still Wants Ottawa to Keep It In." *Globe and Mail* [Toronto] 14 Dec. 1991: A1–2.

Shaw, Brian, comp. *The Gospel According to Saint Pierre*. Richmond Hill, ON: Pocket-Simon, 1969.

Sheppard, Robert, and Michael Valpy. *The National Deal: The Fight for a Canadian Constitution*. Toronto: Macmillan, 1982.

Shugarman, David P., and Reg Whitaker, eds. *Federalism and Political Community: Essays in Honour of Donald Smiley*. Peterborough: Broadview, 1989.

Simpson, Jeffrey. *Faultlines: Struggling for a Canadian Vision*. Toronto: HarperCollins, 1993.

———. *Spoils of Power: The Politics of Patronage*. Don Mills, ON: Collins, 1988.

———. "Trudeau Stands Alone and Defiant." *Globe and Mail* [Toronto] 3 Oct. 1992: A4.

Somerville, David. *Trudeau Revealed by His Actions and Words*. Richmond Hill, ON: BMG, 1978.

Stahl, William A. "Coming to Terms: Defining Structures of Meaning in the Civil Religion and Nationality Debates." *Union Seminary Quarterly Review* 39 (1984): 73–84.

———. "Symbols of Canada: Civil Religion, Nationality, and the

Search for Meaning." Diss. Graduate Theological Union [Berkeley, CA], 1981.

Stanké, Alain. *Pierre Elliott Trudeau: Portrait intime*. Ottawa: Télémetropole; Éditions intl. Alain Stanké, 1977.

Stark, Andrew. "English-Canadian Opposition to Quebec Nationalism." *The Collapse of Canada?* Ed. R. Kent Weaver. Washington, DC: Brookings Inst., 1992. 123–58.

Stewart, Gordon T. *The Origins of Canadian Politics: A Comparative Approach*. Vancouver: U of British Columbia P, 1986.

Stewart, Walter. *Trudeau in Power*. New York: Outerbridge, 1971.

Stuebing, Douglas, with John Marshall and Gary Oakes. *Trudeau: A Man for Tomorrow*. Toronto: Clarke, 1968.

Sullivan, Martin. *Mandate '68*. Toronto: Doubleday, 1968.

Taylor, Charles. *The Pattern of Politics*. Toronto: McClelland, 1970.

——— . *Reconciling the Solitudes: Essays on Canadian Federalism and Nationalism*. Ed. Guy Laforest. Montreal: McGill-Queen's UP, 1993.

——— . "Why Do Nations Have to Become States?" *Philosophers Look at Canadian Confederation / La confédération canadienne: Qu'en pensent les philosophes?* Ed. Stanley G. French. Montreal: Canadian Philos. Assn., 1979. 19–35.

"A Teaser Teased." *Maclean's* 13 Sept. 1993: 37.

Thomson, Dale C. *Jean Lesage and the Quiet Revolution*. Toronto: Macmillan, 1984.

Trofimenkoff, Susan Mann. *The Dream of Nation: A Social and Intellectual History of Quebec*. Toronto: Gage, 1983.

"Trudeau en libraire dès novembre." *Le devoir* [Montréal] 3 sept. 1993: A-2.

Trudeau, Margaret. *Beyond Reason*. New York: Pocket-Simon, 1979.

——— . *Consequences*. Toronto: Seal-McClelland-Bantam, 1982.

Trudeau, Pierre Elliott. "Against Nationalism." *New Perspectives Quarterly* 7.3 (1990): 60–61.

——— . *Approaches to Politics*. Trans. I.M. Owen. Toronto: Oxford UP, 1970.

——— . *The Best of Trudeau: A Compendium of Whimsical Wit and Querulous Quip by Canada's Putative Prince*. Toronto: Modern Canadian Library, 1972.

——— . "Canadian and American Friendship: Canada's Unity Will Not Be Fractured." *Vital Speeches of the Day* 15 Mar. 1977: 322–24.

———. *Conversation with Canadians.* Toronto: U of Toronto P, 1972.

———, ed. *Energy for a Habitable World: A Call for Action.* New York: Crane Russak, 1991.

———. "Exhaustion and Fulfilment: The Ascetic in a Canoe." *Wilderness Canada.* Ed. Borden Spears. Toronto: Clarke, 1970. 3–5.

———. *Fatal Tilt: Speaking Out about Sovereignty.* Point of View Pamphlet Series. Toronto: HarperCollins, 1991.

———. *Federalism and the French Canadians.* Trans. Patricia Claxton and Joanne L'Heureux. New York: St. Martin's, 1968.

———. "Federalism, Nationalism, and Reason." *The Future of Canadian Federalism / L'avenir du fédéralisme canadien.* Ed. P.-A. Crépeau and C.B. MacPherson. Toronto: U of Toronto P; Montréal: P de l'U de Montréal, 1965. 16–35.

———. *Le fédéralisme et la société canadienne-française.* Montréal: Éditions HMH, 1967.

———. *Lifting the Shadow of War.* Ed. C. David Crenna. Edmonton: Hurtig, 1987.

———. "The Meech Lake Accord: Nothing Left But Tears for Trudeau." *Globe and Mail* [Toronto] 28 May 1987: A7.

———. "Meech Lake: End of the Peaceable Kingdom?" *Reader's Digest* [Canada] Aug. 1988: 25–29.

———. *Memoirs.* Toronto: McClelland, 1993.

———. "*A Mess That Deserves a Big No.*" Trans. George Tombs. Toronto: Robert Davies, 1992.

———. "The Multi-National State in Canada." *Canadian Forum* June 1962: 52–54.

———. "New Treason of the Intellectuals." Trudeau, *Federalism* 151–81.

———. "La Nouvelle trahison des clercs." Trudeau, *Le fédéralisme* 159–90.

———. "Peace and Security." *Atlantic Community Quarterly* 21 (1983–84): 301–07.

———. "Postscript: The Poverty of Nationalist Thinking in Quebec." Axworthy and Trudeau, rev. ed. 430–41.

———. "The Practice and Theory of Federalism." *Social Purpose for Canada.* Ed. Michael Oliver. Toronto: U of Toronto P, 1961. 371–93.

———. "La province de Québec au moment de la grève." *La grève de l'amiante.* Ed. Trudeau. 1956. Montréal: Éditions du jour, 1970. 1–91.

———. "The Province of Quebec at the Time of the Strike." *The Asbestos Strike*. Ed. Trudeau. Trans. James Boake. Toronto: James, 1974. 1–82.

———. "Quebec and the Constitutional Problem." Trudeau, *Federalism* 3–51.

———. "Québec et le problème constitutionnel." Trudeau, *Le fédéralisme* 7–59.

———. " 'Say Goodbye to the Dream of One Canada.' " Johnston, *With a Bang* 8–22.

———. "Separatist Counter-Revolutionaries." *Canadian Forum* July 1964: 76–78.

———. "Les séparatistes des contre-révolutionnaires." Trudeau, *Le fédéralisme* 217–27.

———. "Some Obstacles to Democracy in Quebec." *Canadian Journal of Economics and Political Science* 24 (1958): 297–311.

———. " 'There Must Be a Sense of Belonging.' " Johnston, *With a Bang* 23–35.

———. *Trudeau en direct*. Montréal: Éditions du jour, 1972.

———. "Trudeau Speaks Out: The Former Leader Attacks Quebec Nationalists and English Canadians Who Support Them." *Maclean's* 28 Sept. 1992: 22–26.

———. "The Values of a Just Society." Axworthy and Trudeau 357–85.

———. " 'We, the People of Canada.' " Johnston, *With a Bang* 36–105.

Valpy, Michael. "A Myth Remains: A Nation of Losers." *Globe and Mail* [Toronto] 10 July 1990: A5.

———. "Toward a Redefinition of Canada's Mythology." *Globe and Mail* [Toronto] 9 July 1990: A3.

Vastel, Michel. *Bourassa*. Trans. Hubert Bauch. Toronto: Macmillan, 1991.

———. *The Outsider: The Life of Pierre Elliott Trudeau*. Trans. Hubert Bauch. Toronto: Macmillan, 1990.

———. *Trudeau le québécois*. Montréal: Éditions de l'Homme, 1989.

Vear, Danny. "Trudeau a toujours la main (et le pied) agile." *Le devoir* [Montréal] 2 sept. 1993: A-3.

Vienneau, David. "Commons Okays Meech Accord for Second Time." *Toronto Star* 23 June 1988: A9.

Vigod, Bernard L. *Quebec before Duplessis: The Political Career of Louis-Alexandre Taschereau.* Montreal: McGill-Queen's UP, 1986.

"Voices of the Nation: Prominent Canadians Reveal Their Positions for the Oct. 26 Referendum." *Maclean's* 19 Oct. 1992: 22–23.

Wells, Clyde. "Canadians Are Rejecting the Dismantling of Federalism." *Globe and Mail* [Toronto] 14 Apr. 1990: D1–2.

Westell, Anthony. *Paradox: Trudeau as Prime Minister.* Scarborough: Prentice, 1972.

Whitaker, Reg. *A Sovereign Idea: Essays on Canada as a Democratic Community.* Montreal: McGill-Queen's UP, 1992.

Wiles, Peter. "Soviet Economics." *Soviet Studies* [Glasgow] 4 (1952): 133–38.

Wilson, W.A. *The Trudeau Question: Election 1972, an Exclusive Pre-Election Report.* Montreal: *Montreal Star*, 1972.

Wilson-Smith, Anthony. " 'A Great Step for Quebec.' " *Maclean's* 11 May 1987: 12.

Wilson-Smith, Anthony, and Michael Rose. "Breakthrough." *Maclean's* 11 May 1987: 8–10.

Wilson-Smith, Anthony, et al. "On the Rock: The Epic Battle over Meech Lake Leaves a Nation Weakened by Its Own Divisions." *Maclean's* 18 June 1990: 16–21.

Winsor, Hugh. "Trudeau Sings Old Tune." *Globe and Mail* [Toronto] 22 Sept. 1992: A1–2.

Wood, Chris. "Special Report: The Meech Lake Deal." *Maclean's* 20 Mar. 1989: 32–33.

Woods, Shirley E. *Her Excellency, Jeanne Sauvé.* Toronto: Macmillan, 1986.

York, Geoffrey. "Manitoba MLA Throws Meech into Jeopardy: Former Cree Chief Finds Technical Error, Blocks Accord from House until Monday." *Globe and Mail* [Toronto] 15 June 1990: A1, A4.

Zink, Lubor J. *Trudeaucracy.* Toronto: *Toronto Sun*, 1972.

———. *Viva Chairman Pierre.* Toronto: Griffin House, 1977.

Zolf, Larry. *Dance of the Dialectic: How Pierre Elliott Trudeau Went from Philosopher-King to . . . Mackenzie King and Even Better.* Toronto: James, 1973.

———. *Just Watch Me: Remembering Pierre Trudeau.* Toronto: Lorimer, 1984.